THE CLASSICS SLACKER READS
MOBY DICK

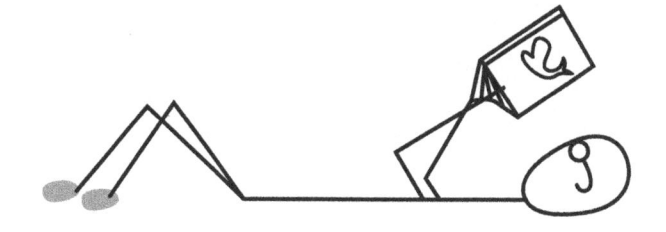

Copyright © 2018 by Cristina Negrón
Second Edition
ISBN: 9781720054849

Illustrations by Kris Wraight
Designed by tslapointedesign.com
"Slacky" drawing by Eliza B.
Text by Cristina Negrón

The Classics Slacker gratefully acknowledges the original Slacker fans (the Slackies) for their steadfast support and encouragement: Amby Burfoot, Olivia Negrón, Sara Pritchard, Deb Martin, Jen Van Allen, and Michelle Hamilton.

"I grin at thee, thou grinning whale!"—STUBB

CONTENTS

Introduction **1**

1. Meet and Greet **4**
2. Sleeping with the Cannibal **6**
3. Calm before the Storm **9**
4. Showboating **12**
5. Dearly Beloved **15**
6. Mmm, Mmm, Good! **18**
7. Ishmael Gets Laid **20**
8. Greet and Eat **23**
9. Only Christians Need Apply **26**
10. No Explanation Needed **29**
11. Beyond All Seasoning **32**
12. The Boys in the Boat **34**
13. Call Him Ahab **37**
14. School of Whales **39**
15. "I'll Take Whales for $100, Alex" **42**
16. Pole Dancing **46**
17. Breaking News **49**
18. Exhale and Inwhale **51**
19. Dancing Queens **53**
20. You Don't Know Dick **56**
21. A Whiter Shade of Whale **59**
22. Ahab's Men-o-pause **62**

23. Case Closed **65**
24. Razzle-Dazzle 'Em **67**
25. The More the Merrier **70**
26. Just Say Row **73**
27. Ishmael Gets Wet **76**
28. Once Upon a Midnight Dreary **79**
29. Like Ships Passing **82**
30. The Town-Ho's Story **85**
31. Ho **87**
32. Ho, Ho **90**
33. Ho, Ho, Ho **93**
34. "But I Digress" **96**
35. The Subplots Thicken **99**
36. Sperm! Sperm! Sperm! **104**
37. Fish and Ships **107**
38. "If I Were a Carpenter" **112**
39. Let's Call the Whole Thing Off **115**
40. Last Gasps **118**
Postscript **121**

The Obligatory Author Biography **122**

INTRODUCTION

Remember the Mayans? Remember when they predicted the world was going to end on December 12, 2012? When I heard that, my first thought was, "Oh my god! I never read *Moby Dick!*"

I planned to read it someday, of course—and lots of other classic books. I didn't know I had a specific and literal deadline. So as the clock ticked down to doomsday, I opened up *Moby Dick* and started reading. Fell asleep right after "Call me Ishmael."

When I woke up on December 13, 2012—noticing that I and the world still existed—I rolled over and went back to sleep. Five years later I still hadn't read *Moby Dick*. I had to face the truth: I was a classics slacker. The Classics Slacker.

Maybe you're a classics slacker, too. Here's how to tell: When you come across those lists of "100 Greatest Books of All Time," are you shocked to discover that you've only read three? Or maybe you've read ten, but can't remember anything except carriage rides, bonnets, and couples exchanging meaningful glances over embroidery.

Anyway, if this sounds like you, and it probably does, you will likely respond in one of two ways:

- With shame and self-loathing (especially if you were an English major, as was The Classics Slacker). To cope with these feelings, you pour a large glass of wine and, instead of reading something—anything—you watch *When Harry Met Sally* for the 103rd time.

- With renewed ambition. You drive to your nearest used bookstore and buy a pile of classic novels such as *Ulysses, War and Peace, A Tale of Two Cities, Madame Bovary,*

Wuthering Heights, etc., etc., etc. (That's the Latin abbreviation for "Wow, how many of these books are there, anyway?") Back home, you slide them onto your bookshelf, assuming you have one. There they will taunt you every day, increasing your already *Les Misérables*-sized self-contempt to the height and width of the British Library.

But no more, my fellow well-intentioned, literature-impaired friends! There is another way! The Classics Slacker is reading the classics so you don't have to. No longer will you feel unworthy every time you encounter a list of "Books You Should Have Read or You Are an Idiot."

One of those books is invariably *Moby Dick,* long chosen by high school students everywhere as the most detested novel in the history of literature. For that reason alone, it is the first selection in *The Classics Slacker* series.

Written by American novelist Herman Melville, *Moby Dick* was published in 1851. Reading was one of only two forms of indoor entertainment back then; the other was attending parties where you were forced to listen to the host's teenage daughter play the pianoforte for hours.

Nonetheless, Melville's novel was not well received. Just about everyone hated it. Especially the parts about whales, which, sad to say, make up large portions of the book.

Despite its lackluster launch, *Moby Dick* ranks way up there among the greatest books of all time. It's certainly the fishiest. True, some scholars argue for Ernest Hemingway's *The Old Man and the Sea*. But *Dick* is seven times longer than *Old Man,* and whales are way bigger than marlin. Thus, The Classics Slacker must give the nod to *Dick*.

You might have noticed that The Classics Slacker spells *Moby Dick* without a hyphen. It often appears with a hyphen. The Classics Slacker has meticulously researched this hyphen/no

INTRODUCTION

hyphen question and still hasn't reached a definitive conclusion. The decision to go hyphenless in this volume was made really only to save ink.

With or without a hyphen, *Moby Dick* has 135 chapters. Among them: "Of the Less Erroneous Pictures of Whales, and the True Pictures of Whaling Scenes"; "The Great Heidelburgh Tun"; "Ambergris"; "A Bower in the Arsacides"; and "Measurement of the Whale's Skeleton."

By comparison, *The Classics Slacker Reads Moby Dick* has only forty chapters (along with cute illustrations). Among them: "Ishmael Gets Laid"; "Call Him Ahab"; "You Don't Know Dick"; "A Whiter Shade of Whale"; and "Sperm! Sperm! Sperm!"

Which book would you rather read?

The Classics Slacker couldn't agree more.

1
MEET AND GREET

*In which Ishmael calls himself Ishmael
and invites everyone else to do the same*

The first sentence of *Moby Dick* goes down real easy, like swallowing a goldfish. After all, it's only three words: "Call me Ishmael."

The second sentence isn't too bad, either, although considerably longer (forty words). Basically Ishmael says he's decided to go out to sea. He says when he feels depressed—or as Ishmael puts it "a damp, drizzly November in my soul"—he figures it's time to head for the water.

Who can't relate to this? Beyond lifting moods, the sights and sounds of the ocean can silence mindless brain chatter. Notes Ishmael: "Meditation and water are wedded forever." Or, as The Classics Slacker's mom used to say, "I do my best thinking in the bathtub." That works pretty well, too, if you can't get to the ocean.

Poor Ishmael can't afford a bathtub or a boat ride. But that's okay with him. He prefers to get a job on a ship. "Passengers get sea-sick—grow quarrelsome—don't sleep of nights—do not enjoy themselves much, as a general thing;—no I never go as a passenger."

Smart guy. Having once endured the horrors of a cruise vacation, The Classics Slacker understands completely.

But before Ishmael can find a ship he can work for, he has to fish around for a place to stay for a couple nights in New Bedford, Massachusetts, because he missed the boat (ha!) out of Nantucket: "For my mind was made up to sail in no other than a Nantucket craft, because there was a fine, boisterous something about everything connected with that famous old island, which amazingly pleased me."

Ishmael would love to check into one of New Bedford's top-rated hotels on Trip Advisor, but he lacks the cash: "With anxious grapnels I had sounded my pocket and only brought up a few pieces of silver." Before he books a room, he advises himself to "be sure to inquire the price, and don't be too particular."

If his finances were a bit healthier, he might have stayed at The Crossed Harpoons. But from the street it looked "too expensive and jolly." Same problem with The Sword-Fish Inn, also "too expensive and jolly." Ishmael needs someplace cheap and depressing. At last he happens upon The Spouter-Inn. "As the swinging sign had a poverty-stricken sort of creak to it, I thought that here was the very spot for cheap lodgings."

In other words, perfect!

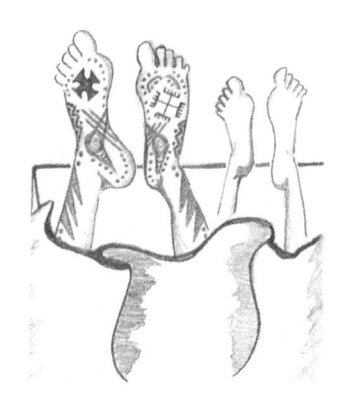

2
SLEEPING WITH THE CANNIBAL

In which Ishmael's hotel room comes with a rather bizarre amenity

Our guy Ishmael has a problem of biblical proportions. There are no rooms left at the Inn. But the innkeeper—Peter Coffin—has a ready solution: Ishmael can bunk down with one of his regular boarders, a harpooneer named Queequeg. There's just one little issue with it—the room has only one bed.

Ishmael has some misgivings about this proposition: "No man prefers to sleep two in a bed...And when it comes to sleeping with an unknown stranger in a strange inn, in a strange town, and that stranger a harpooneer, then your objections indefinitely multiply."

Mr. Coffin offers Ishmael a bench to sleep on and hauls out his woodworking tools to try to make it as comfortable as, well, a coffin. Soon wood shavings are flying all over the place. "The landlord was near spraining his wrist, and I told him for heaven's sake to quit—the bed was soft enough to suit me, and I did not know how all the planing in the world could make eider down of a pine plank."

Ishmael decides to take his chances with the harpooneer after all, who has yet to show up. Peter Coffin reassures him all will be well. "He pays reg'lar," says the innkeeper, admitting that Queequeg supplements his harpooneer's income by selling shrunken heads on the side.

Ishmael, pooped, troops upstairs to his room. He gets into bed, curls himself into the fetal position, and nearly reaches "the land of Nod."

Then Queequeg enters the room. He does not slip in unnoticed. First off, he's huge, bald, and covered in tats. Ishmael's eyes pop open at the sight of him. He tries to rationalize away Queequeg's appearance: "It's only his outside; a man can be honest in any sort of skin."

True. But the shrunken heads salesman is also smoking "great clouds of tobacco," toting his inventory, and waving a tomahawk. For some reason, Ishmael hadn't put together that selling heads and cannibalism go hand in hand (the best parts). He is stunned speechless, overcome with fear. Queequeg finally notices the mute Ishmael when he climbs into bed.

Screaming ensues until Peter Coffin rushes in to save the day (night). He clears up the confusion between the two men, and Ishmael sees that Queequeg means no harm. "For all his tattooings he was on the whole a clean, comely looking cannibal." And he had seen earlier in the evening how destructive arrantest topers (drunk sailors) can be. He decides, rather philosophically, "Better sleep with a sober cannibal than a drunken Christian."

Cannibals, sure. But smokers, no. That's where Ishmael draws the line, and Queequeg kindly agrees to extinguish his smoking materials. "I don't fancy having a man smoking in bed with me," Ishmael says. "It's dangerous. Besides, I ain't insured."

If only Ishmael lived in Canada instead of the United States. He would've been covered by universal health care.

3
CALM BEFORE THE STORM

In which Ishmael is bored by sleepy sailors at The Spouter-Inn

Melville knows a thing or two about pacing. First he riles up his reader with the exciting tale of Ishmael and his new cannibalistic bedfellow, Queequeg. Once his reader realizes that Ishmael survives the night without getting eaten (which would make for a much shorter book), the author slows things down a bit and gives his reader a chance to breathe. But perhaps Melville slows things down a bit too much. The Classics Slacker was in danger of dozing.

Because, over the next ten pages or so, Ishmael recounts a series of his doings where he's doing nothing. He wakes up next to Queequeg. He watches Queequeg get dressed. He eats breakfast. He walks around New Bedford. Yawn.

Wasn't Ishmael supposed to go on some sort of voyage? Yes, indeed. Back on page 1, there it is: "I thought I would sail about a little bit and see the watery part of the world." Then why the dressing, the eating, the walking?

Who knows? Apparently, Ishmael thinks this is interesting stuff. Regarding Queequeg's morning routine: "At that time in the morning any Christian would have washed his face; but Queequeg, to my amazement contented himself with restricting his ablutions to his chest, arms, and hands."

If anything's amazing it's that Ishmael is captivated by all this. At least he knows he's being a bit of a weirdo and not as cultured as the cannibal. "He treated me with so much consideration, while I was guilty of a great rudeness; staring at him from the bed, and watching all his toilette motions; for the time my curiosity getting the better of my breeding."

Breakfast is boring, too, as the rowdy sailors of the previous evening sit mute before their coffee and hot rolls. Ishmael had thought breakfast would be an entertaining affair, that he would "hear some good stories about whaling." But none are forthcoming. "To my no small surprise nearly every man maintained a profound silence." Why? He doesn't say. But it's almost certainly because their heads are pounding with massive hangovers.

So Ishmael leaves the inn to stroll around New Bedford. Nothing's really happening there, either, until he goes to Whaleman's Chapel.

And then, finally...something of interest. Within the walls of the chapel Ishmael reads marble memorials of dead men "lost overboard," "towed out of sight by a whale," "killed by a Sperm Whale" etc., etc. "It needs scarcely to be told *[which of course means he's going to tell us anyway]*, with what feelings, on the eve of a Nantucket voyage *[yippee, there is a voyage coming at some point, maybe even tomorrow]* I regarded those marble tablets, and by the murky light of that darkened, doleful day read the fate of the whalemen who had gone before me."

In sum, the memorials cause Ishmael to think "hmmm." But not to worry. Although he knows he may die at sea, he calls it "a speechlessly quick chaotic bundling of man into Eternity." As opposed to a slow orderly dying of reader by boredom.

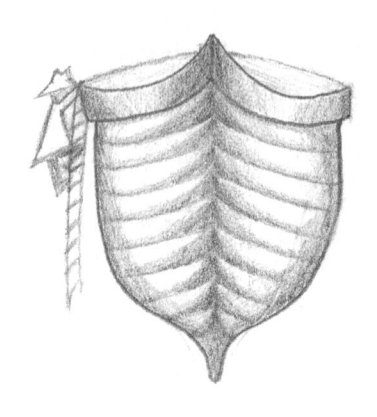

4
SHOWBOATING

In which the Whaleman's Chapel pastor delivers the "Jonah and the Whale" sermon for the sixty-five millionth time

When the name of a church is "Whaleman's Chapel," you can bet your fish and chips that the dominant décor is "Naturally Nautical." The Whaleman's Chapel does not disappoint. Dead sailor memorials and gigantic paintings of sinking ships festoon the walls. A pulpit, fashioned in the likeness of a ship's bow, towers above the pews.

The Classics Slacker thinks the pulpit, as described by Ishmael, seems a tad over the top for a humble house of worship, but our narrator defends it: "The whole contrivance, considering what manner of chapel it was, seemed by no means in bad taste." Perhaps. But it's definitely impractical. Ishmael wonders how the pulpiteer (Father Mapple) is going to deliver a sermon from that height, especially since the pulpit lacks an obvious means of ascent. Then he sees it: "The architect, it seemed, had acted upon the hint of Father Mapple, and finished the pulpit without a stairs, substituting a perpendicular side ladder, like those used in mounting a ship from a boat at sea."

Ishmael also reports that "the wife of a whaling captain had provided the chapel with a handsome pair of red worsted man-ropes for this ladder." Which makes The Classics Slacker question how in the name of Long John Silver does Ishmael have so much insider information about the construction of the pulpit? Maybe he happened to sit next to the wife of the whaling captain and she said, "Hey, you. You're new here, right? Guess what? I provided that handsome pair of red worsted man-ropes for the ladder."

Anyway, once Father Mapple makes his entrance, sleet dripping from his Gorton Fisherman's hat, Ishmael can tell that he'll have no problem climbing the rope ladder. He notes that the vigorous pastor is in "the hardy winter of a healthy old age." And indeed he climbs up with no difficulty whatsoever.

Now situated in the pulpit, Father Fitness appears ready to pontificate, but his parishioners haven't quite settled down. They've seen this rope-climbing trick dozens of times, and it doesn't impress them the way it transfixes Ishmael. So the pastor has to call them to attention, which he does thusly: "Starboard gangway, there! Side away to larboard—larboard gangway to starboard! Midships! midships!"

Now, The Classics Slacker was dragged to a few Catholic masses as a child and witnessed some weird stuff. But the Catholic priest knew that his congregants were sitting in pews, not standing ready to jib the sails (or whatever you call it; The Classics Slacker knows nothing about boats). This Father Mapple seems to have lost his oyster crackers.

Strangely, Mapple's minions know that "larboarding the gangway to starboard" means sit down and shut up. Father Mapple "slowly turns over the leaves of the Bible," apparently looking for the parable du jour. But he's really just milking every second, trying to build up dramatic tension because he chooses (surprise!): Jonah and the Whale!

His parishioners, living as they do in New Bedford, Massachusetts, no doubt have heard this story as often as foghorns. Nonetheless, they larboard themselves to starboard and listen to Father Mapple drone on for the next seven pages.

The Classics Slacker would've definitely jumped overboard.

5
DEARLY BELOVED

In which Ishmael and Queequeg take their relationship to a whole new level

If same-sex marriage had been legal in 1850, Ishmael and Queequeg would've gone straight to the wedding registry at Bed, Bath, and Beyond.

The relationship of these two lovebirds develops like the plot of a modern rom-com. Thrown together by fate at the Spouter-Inn—where they are forced to spend the night together in one bed—Ishmael is repulsed by the sight of Queequeg. At first. But soon he finds himself intrigued by Queequeg's tats, his "bald purplish head," and his nighttime routine, which includes saying prayers to a wooden idol.

By morning Ishmael discovers Queequeg's arm "wrapped around me in the most loving and affectionate manner. You had almost thought I had been his wife." Almost? He "hugged me tightly, as though not but death should part us twain."

Ishmael attempts to "unlock his bridegroom's grasp." He's not *that* easy, after all. He has to be wooed and won. In every love story one partner is always a little reluctant. Otherwise the story would be over in ten minutes.

Ishmael begins to observe Queequeg with increasing interest—and affection. After attending the sermon at the Whaleman's Chapel, Ishmael returns to the Spouter-Inn and notices Queequeg trying to read a book. Ishmael continues to watch his roommate surreptitiously, "half-pretending" that he's just looking out the windows. He is touched to see the cannibal trying to educate himself—even though he's just turning pages, not comprehending anything, and stops at page 50. This, coincidentally, is about the same place where The Classics Slacker wanted to give up on *Moby Dick*.

But back to our lovers. As Ishmael continues to gaze at Queequeg, a surprising revelation comes over him: "Through all his unearthly tattooings, I thought I saw the traces of a simple honest heart; and in his large, deep eyes, fiery black and bold, there seemed tokens of a spirit that would dare a thousand devils." This guy is clearly falling in love. Indeed, just a page later, Ishmael confesses: "I began to be sensible of strange feelings. I felt a melting in me."

What follows is a typical lovers' montage: Ish and Double Q (their pet names) overcoming their language barrier, smoking in bed together (apparently Ishmael no longer cares about risk of fire), taking little naps (Queequeg "now and then affectionately throwing his brown tattooed legs over mine"), eating cozy dinners for two, discussing religion, more smoking in bed.

All this time in bed naturally leads to pillow talk. And so, Queequeg tells Ishmael his life story. Turns out, ta-da! he's not just a regular old cannibal. He's the son of a king! Ishmael's prince has come.

And so, the two are wed. "He pressed his forehead against

mine, clasped me round the waist, and said that henceforth we were married." Afterward they engage in the most intimate act a couple can share: divvying up their money. "He drew out some thirty dollars in silver; then spreading them on the table, and mechanically dividing them into two equal portions, pushed one of them towards me, and said it was mine." Wow, Queequeg, The Classics Slacker hopes you asked Ishmael to sign a prenup.

At last Queequeg and Ishmael sail for Nantucket—sort of a honeymoon cruise. On the ship Queequeg dives into the water to save a jerk who goes overboard. It's a real turn-on to see your beloved risk his life in a brave rescue, and with such humility. Says Ishmael: "He did not seem to think that he at all deserved a medal from the Humane and Magnanimous Societies." Ishmael is permanently and forever bound to his man. "From that hour I clove to Queequeg like a barnacle."

If only they really could've married. "Cannibal and Barnacle, do you take each other to be your lawfully wedded husbands?"

They do!

6

MMM, MMM, GOOD!

In which Mrs. Hosea Hussey serves up some mighty tasty chowdah to a salivating Ishmael and Queequeg

Ishmael and Queequeg love soup. What kind? Chowder, of course. We discover just how much they love chowder in a chapter Melville calls "Chowder," where we pick up our tale.

Hungry as all get out, the newlyweds stumble into the Try Pots Inn, owned by Peter Coffin's cousin Hosea Hussey. Evidently restaurant and hotel management runs in the family.

Ishmael asks the proprietress, Mrs. Hussey, for supper, to which she barks, "Clam or Cod?" Ishmael politely asks for more details about the fish: "What's that about Cods, ma'am?" Is it grilled, fried, breaded? Mrs. Hussey refuses to elaborate and instead repeats her question like an exasperated diner waitress: "Clam or Cod?"

Ishmael is alarmed. "A clam for supper?" he asks. "A cold clam: is that what you mean, Mrs. Hussey? But that's a rather cold and clammy reception in the winter time, ain't it, Mrs. Hussey?" He and Queequeg are starving; he's hoping the clam comes with a side order of fries and coleslaw at least. Mrs. Hussey is in no mood to discuss the house specials. After hearing Ishmael say "clam" three times, she bolts for the kitchen and yells to the cook, "Clam for two."

Panic sets in: "Queequeg, do you think that we can make out a supper for us both on one clam?" They *would* need a pretty small fork.

No need to strategize as it turns out. This clam/cod business is just a comical miscommunication, as most miscommunications are. Mrs. Hussey brings each of them a bowl of clam chowder worthy of Emeril's. Chowder is the specialty of the house—the only specialty of the house. What Mrs. Hussey failed to explain is that the Try Pots Inn serves two kinds of chowder—clam and cod. When Ishmael said "clam," Mrs. Hussey brought them clam chowder. After finishing up the clam chowder, they order "cod," and Mrs. Hussey brings them cod chowder. They have cracked the cod, er, code.

Ishmael and Queequeg go on to chow down on chowder for breakfast, lunch, and dinner. Doesn't seem to bother those two chowderheads. Not one clam. Or cod.

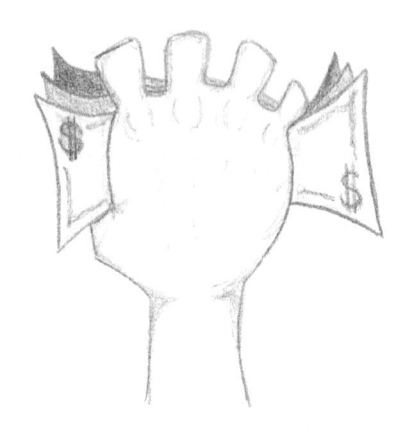

7
ISHMAEL GETS LAID

In which our hero barters his brawny body for a goodly price to the whaling ship Pequod

Lots of couples talk over their plans in bed, and Ishmael and Queequeg are no exception. "In bed we concocted our plan for the morrow." First on the agenda: choose a ship for their big adventure. It's no small decision; they'll be spending the next 430 pages on this particular boat. Even so, Queequeg says Ishmael must go ship shopping by himself.

See, Queequeg has consulted his adviser, Yojo, about the matter. Yojo is kind of like Yoda. Perhaps George Lucas modeled Yoda after Yojo. After all, *Moby Dick* preceded *Star Wars* by 127 years. And the characters look suspiciously similar. Yojo is "a curious little deformed image with a hunch on his back."

Yojo doesn't talk out loud (he's made of wood), but Queequeg receives his messages loud and clear. On this subject, Yojo has said something like: "Ship you will choose not with Ishmael, ehm."

ISHMAEL GETS LAID

Knowing Queequeg would never disobey Yoda, er, Yojo, Ishmael heads to the shipyard alone and checks out a few vessels. He quickly dismisses the *Devil-Dam* and the *Tit-Bit*, based on their names alone one assumes. And then, like Goldilocks, Ishmael climbs aboard the *Pequod* and declares her just right.

The first guy he sees hanging out on the *Pequod* is a dude named Peleg. Ishmael assumes he's the ship's captain. But it turns out Peleg and his buddy Bildad are part owners. Ishmael has to interview with them before landing a whale-hunting job.

Peleg and Bildad subject Ishmael to all the standard interview questions: Have you ever gone whaling before? Where do you see yourself in five years? Do you like seafood?

Ishmael answers the questions satisfactorily, and so the three of them move on to the next stage: salary negotiation.

Whalemen are paid by getting laid. Or rather, they are ranked by the way they lay. Meaning, the higher your lay ranking, the more money you earn; a lay is a percentage of the ship's earnings. It's all very democratic. Naturally the guys on top get the best lay.

Bildad decides that Ishmael is worth the 777th lay. Peleg is shocked by his partner's paltry offer and a little embarrassed, too. "Why, blast your eyes, Bildad! Thou dost not want to swindle this young man! He must have more than that." Peleg ups it to 300. This makes Ishmael a lot happier, even though he had been hoping for 275, maybe even 200, "considering I was of a broad-shouldered make."

Our hero thinks the deal is sealed, but then finds out that he still has to pass muster with the big boss, the captain of the *Pequod*: Ahab.

Ishmael hasn't heard great things about Ahab. But Peleg does his best to quell his anxiety. Sure, Ahab's been "kind of moody" since the last voyage when a whale "devoured, chewed up, and crunched his leg." But who wouldn't be?

Ishmael decides to put his trust in Peleg. After all, Peleg was the one who gave him a good lay.

8
GREET AND EAT

Queequeg introduces Ishmael to Ramadan, which includes long-lasting fasting and occasional same-species feasting

At times, *Moby Dick* is laugh-out-loud funny. Seriously. The Classics Slacker laughed out loud.

Take the chapter called "The Ramadan" where Queequeg observes, you guessed it, Ramadan. (Melville has a real flair for chapter titles.) Although Ishmael practices Christianity and Queequeg practices Cannibalism (the food is better), Ishmael is surprisingly tolerant. On their first night together he says, "Better sleep with a sober cannibal than a drunken Christian." He even tries to understand Queequeg's religion. "Although I applied myself to it several times, I never could master his liturgies." In other words, Ishmael just doesn't "get" Ramadan.

Still, when the holy day arrives, Ishmael leaves Queequeg alone so he can fast and meditate. He last sees him "posed on his hams in a cold room, holding a piece of wood on his head." The "wood," as the ham-headed Ishmael refers to it, is Queequeg's beloved idol, Yojo. (See "Ishmael Gets Laid" on page 20 for more about Yojo.)

Ishmael does not expect Queequeg's observance of Ramadan to last longer than your typical Catholic mass, where, it must be pointed out, celebrants crunch wafer cookies made of body parts and drink wine distilled from blood. (Who's the cannibal now?) But Ishmael is about to learn that a Ramadan meditation, at least the cannibal version, outlasts most, if not all, of your major religious services. When Ishmael returns, he finds the door locked. He knocks. No answer. He yells. No answer. He grows frantic, imagining that his "friend" (see "Dearly Beloved" on page 15 for the truth about these two) has had a stroke, or worse.

Ishmael runs for help and finds the mistress of the house, Mrs. Hussey. She discovers Queequeg's harpoon missing from the storage closet, confirming Ishmael's worst fear. She is none too pleased about it, either. "It will be the ruin of my house," she gripes. "Betty," she commands her chambermaid, "Go to Snarles the painter and tell him to paint me a sign: 'No suicides permitted here, and no smoking in the parlor.' Might as well kill both birds at once." Too bad Mrs. Hussey hadn't posted that sign earlier. It might have saved Queequeg's life—and lots of money on upholstery cleaning.

Ishmael takes matters into his own hands, literally, and breaks down the door. He finds Queequeg very much alive but still locked in Ramadan-meditation mode. "Queequeg! *[paraphrasing]* What's the matter with you?" gripes an exasperated Ishmael. No answer. "He would not move a peg, nor say a single word, nor notice my presence in any the slightest way."

So Ishmael replies, in short, "Okay, have it your way" and stalks out. He probably would've slammed the door, too, if there still was one.

By 11 p.m., Ishmael has cooled off. "I went up stairs to go

GREET AND EAT

to bed, feeling quite sure by this time Queequeg must certainly have brought his Ramadan to a termination. But no; there he was just where I left him; he had not stirred an inch."

Ishmael endures a restless night. "Think of it; sleeping all night in the same room with a wide awake pagan on his hams, stark alone in the cold and dark; this made me really wretched."

Finally, upon the first light of dawn, Queequeg gets up, "with stiff and grating joints" but smiling, nonetheless. "He limped towards me where I lay; pressed his forehead again against mine; and said his Ramadan was over."

Not so Ishmael's scolding. He calls Queequeg's observance of Ramadan "stark nonsense; bad for the health; useless for the soul; opposed to the obvious laws of common sense." Worst of all, he claims, "fasting makes the body cave in" and causes "dyspepsia."

On this last point Queequeg must disagree. He tells Ishmael that only once in his life did he suffer from dyspepsia (fancy word for an upset stomach). And it wasn't caused by fasting. Quite the opposite. He tells Ishmael of a "memorable" victory feast, when "fifty of the enemy had been killed by about two o'clock in the afternoon, and all cooked and eaten that very evening." That's when he got a tummy ache.

Those cannibals…such cut-ups.

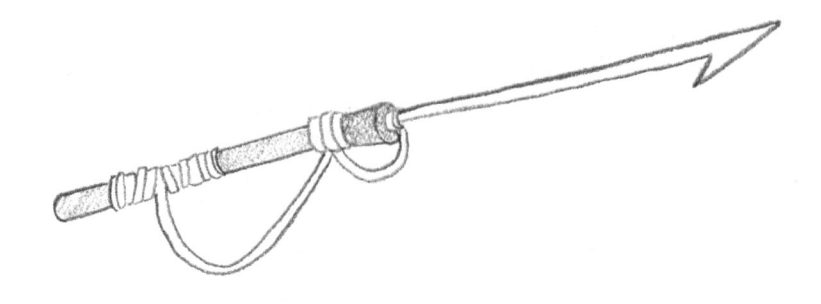

9
ONLY CHRISTIANS NEED APPLY

*In which hypocritical ship owners deny Queequeg a job—
until they watch him hurl a harpoon*

Ishmael thinks he's wrapped up a sweet deal for himself and his sweetheart, Queequeg. (He says they are "just friends," but we know otherwise.) Ishmael has worked out all the details with the *Pequod*'s two-man human resources department—Bildad and Peleg. After an extensive interview (nothing in *Moby Dick* is anything less than extensive), Bildad and Peleg hire Ishmael and agree to bring on Queequeg as well, sight unseen.

Until his sight is seen. Queequeg's tête-to-toes tats betray him immediately as someone who diets on humans (a humanitarian). He might as well have an elbow hanging from his mouth.

Whoa, now wait one minute! Peleg says. We don't want his kind working for us. Unless he can "show his papers." (What is this, Arizona?)

Close. When the whaling bosses demand that you show your

papers, it's not because you look like a Mexican. It's because you don't look like a Christian. Queequeg clearly does not. But if he can show papers proving that he's converted to Christianity, they'll allow him to board the boat.

Of course Queequeg doesn't have papers. He's never been baptized; why it's as obvious as the blue paint on his face. Ishmael tries to persuade Peleg to accept him anyway. He waxes eloquent about how we are all, including Queequeg, children of God. "Every mother's son and soul of us belong; the great and everlasting First Congregation of this whole worshipping world; we all belong to that; only some of us cherish some queer crotchets noways touching the grand belief; in *that* we all join hands."

Very pretty sermon, says Peleg. But no dice. Christianity is an exclusive club and no way are we letting your buddy in unless he has ID.

That is until Peleg espies Queequeg's harpoon. Why that's a mighty impressive stick ya got there, he says. What did you say your name was—Quohog, Queerdog, Hedgehog? Do you know how to use that thing? "Did you ever strike a fish?"

Did Queequeg ever strike a fish? Did Melville ever write an incomprehensible sentence? To answer Peleg's question, Queequeg points to a tar spot on the water and "taking sharp aim at it, he darted the iron right over Bildad's broad brim, clean across the ship's decks, and struck the glistening tar spot out of sight." Little-known fact: Babe Ruth had just finished reading chapter 18 of *Moby Dick* the day he pointed to the stands and homered to that very spot.

"Now," says Queequeg. "Spos-ee him *[meaning the spot]* whale-e eye; why, dad whale dead."

Come again? asks Peleg. But who cares. Queequeg made his point with his pointy harpoon. Suddenly Peleg worships him more than Jesus and hires him on the spot. He even gives him a more lucrative contract than Ishmael's. Bildad isn't quite as ready to trade in his moral principles for money, but Peleg is hooked. "Pious harpooneers never make good voyagers," he argues. "It takes the shark out of them."

Unless, of course, your shark claims to be a Christian. If that happens, demand to see his papers.

10
NO EXPLANATION NEEDED

In which Ishmael defends the profession of whaling for pages and pages while The Classics Slacker begs him to clam up

The deed is done. Queequeg and Ishmael are finally, after 95 pages and 22 chapters, ON THE BOAT. Bildad's sister, Charity, has packed the crew's lunches, sewed their names into their underwear, supplied them with toilet paper, toothpaste, and, almost certainly, condoms. "She seemed resolved that, if she could help it, nothing should be found wanting on the *Pequod*, after once fairly getting to sea." Ishmael has been warned, several times, by a creepy soothsayer (what other kind is there?) not to go. But he ignores the dude, dismissing him as a "humbug, trying to be a bugbear." (At least he's ambitious.) He hasn't yet laid eyes on Captain Ahab, but figures, hey, how bad can he be? Time to push off and set sail! Yes?

No. At this point Ishmael feels compelled to explain to his long-suffering readers—who've really only begun to suffer—why whalemen are just the best. And he means to take five pages to do it.

Really, Ishmael, please don't. (The Classics Slacker has taken to talking to him out loud.) No need to explain. Can you please just continue the story?

No, he says (he's taken to talking back as well), I'm going to tell you and I'm going to tell you good. Now listen up.

People call whalemen butchers, Ishmael says. True, there is a lot of blood involved. But at least we clean up after ourselves. In fact, whaling ships are "among the cleanliest things of this tidy earth." Much cleaner than battlefields. And what do soldiers give you, anyway? he asks. Just a lot of dead guys. Whalemen, on the other hand, give you oil for your lamps. We light up your life. We give you hope, to carry on. We light up your days, and fill your nights, with, song! He's gone all Debby Boone on us.

Besides, he continues, bringing y'all lamp oil is just one service we whalemen provide. We've done so much other good stuff that I'm not even going to try to tell you about them. "It would be a hopeless, endless task to catalogue all these things," he declares. But by now we know Ishmael can't be trusted.

We've charted uncharted territories, he begins. We've fed starving Australians, brainwashed pagan Polynesians, tamed Japanese savages, and liberated Peruvians, Chileans, and Bolivians.

Now, Ishmael says, have I convinced you yet that we are awesome? Yes, Ishmael, you had us at "clean." He doesn't believe us. In fact, he's threatening to clock us: "But if, in the face of all this, you still declare that whaling has no aesthetically noble associations connected with it, then am I ready to shiver fifty lances with you there, and unhorse you with a split helmet every time."

At this point, The Classics Slacker has left the room. So Ishmael debates himself. He actually throws down a series of charges against whalemen and/or whaling and repudiates them

NO EXPLANATION NEEDED

one by one. "Whaling not respectable? Whaling is imperial!" And: "No dignity in whaling! The dignity of our calling the very heavens attest."

And so on. By the fourth or fifth one, he's worked himself up into such a lather that he's about to punch himself in the face. He's never been more furious at himself.

Finally he says, I'm not listening to myself anymore. This conversation is over. Except, it isn't. See next chapter: "Beyond All Seasoning."

11
BEYOND ALL SEASONING

Fun fact! Kings and queens style their hair with Sperm Whale oil before their coronation ceremonies. Eww

Previously, on *Moby Dick*: Ishmael has tied himself into knots, for an entire chapter, arguing in impassioned prose as to why whaling is the greatest gift to the world and all its inhabitants. And why all who engage in whaling should be sanctified.

You'd think Ishmael would be all tuckered out and ready to take a nap, preferably in the arms of Queequeg.

If only. Ishmael isn't through yet. The next chapter is titled: "Postscript" aka "Ishmael Has at Least One More Point to Make."

It begins thusly: "In behalf of the dignity of whaling, I would fain advance naught but substantiated facts *[facts expounded upon in excruciating detail in the last chapter]*. But after embattling his facts *[beating them to death, actually]*, an advocate *[that would be Ishmael, of course]* who should wholly suppress a not unreasonable surmise, which might tell eloquently upon his cause—such an advocate, would he not be blame-worthy?"

Well, yes, he would. But that doesn't stop him.

And so, Ishmael continues. It is "well known," he reports, that before a king or queen's coronation ceremony "a certain curious process of seasoning them" is conducted. With salt. Whether a measuring spoon is employed or if the royals are simply sprinkled to taste, he's not sure. "How they use the salt, precisely—who knows?"

Maybe by sealing the coronee's head in a plastic bag with the salt, bread crumbs, and a little paprika?

What Ishmael does know is that "a king's head is solemnly oiled at his coronation, even as a head of salad."

Is anyone else getting hungry?

Anyway, Ishmael has no tolerance, in any other circumstance, for guys putting stuff in their hair. It's okay for royals but, "In common life we esteem but meanly and contemptibly a fellow who anoints his hair, and palpably smells of that anointing. In truth, a mature man who uses hairoil, that man has probably got a quoggy spot in him somewhere." Probably on his head, one would guess.

But back to our king and his big day. Guess what kind of "hairoil" is used for kings at their coronation? Not olive, not "macassar" (nineteenth-century Brylcreem), not castor, not cod-liver, not canola, not "I Can't Believe It's Not Butter," not WD-40, but, you guessed it: whale oil! And not just any ol' whale oil but "the sperm oil in its unmanufactured, unpolluted state, the sweetest of all oils."

Yes, Ishmael crows, "We whalemen supply your kings and queens with coronation stuff!" So there!

And really, that's way more than needs to be said.

12

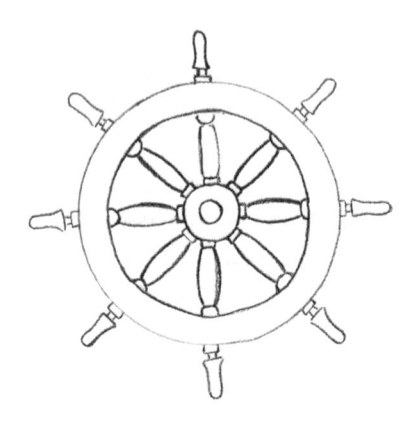

THE BOYS IN THE BOAT

*In which Ishmael describes his future shipmates—
even though he hasn't met them yet*

By page 103, Ishmael and Queequeg are the only two whalers Mr. Melville has explored intimately. Almost as intimately as they've explored each other. But as soon as they climb aboard the *Pequod*, it's clear that we're going to learn more, a lot more, about Ishmael and Queequeg's shipmates to be. Curiously, Ishmael already knows a boatload of details about everybody—work histories, personality traits, habits, turn ons and turn offs—even though he hasn't traveled one nautical mile with any of them.

He begins by describing Starbuck, the first mate, and continues all the way down the line of command over the next several chapters. Mostly he seems obsessed, no surprise, with their bodies. Starbuck's flesh is "hard as a twice baked biscuit" and his "pure tight skin was an excellent fit." Stubb, the second mate, doesn't entice as much as Starbuck. He's second, after all. But

Ishmael has apparently watched him get dressed: "Instead of first putting his legs into his trowsers, he put his pipe into his mouth." He finishes up with a saucy description of the third mate, Little Flask, who is "one of the wrought ones; made to clinch tight and last long."

It gets worse: Each mate gets to choose his very own harpooneer. Naturally these couples develop "a close intimacy and friendliness." Naturally. Starbuck chooses Queequeg (so long, Ishmael) and Stubb picks Tashtego, who has "long, lean, sable hair," "high cheekbones," "black rounding eyes," and "tawny brawn lithe snaky limbs." With the two hottest harpooneers already spoken for, poor Little Flask has to settle for Daggoo, who at least is "erect as a giraffe" and has great taste in jewelry. "Suspended from his ears were two golden hoops, so large that the sailors called them ringbolts."

The rest of the crew is hardly worth mentioning. Ishmael calls them "residue." They're just the brawn while the Americans—Starbuck, Stubb, and Flask (from Nantucket, Cape Cod, and Martha's Vineyard, respectively)—are the brains.

Stuck at the bottom, the *Pequod*'s equivalent of the mailroom, is the steward: Dough-Boy. Really? His parents named him Dough-Boy? The only explanation is that when he was a baby, his parents ("a bankrupt banker and a hospital nurse") poked his tummy and he giggled. Cute then, not so useful now. Now he's condemned to a life of serving crescent rolls to a bunch of bullies who knock him around as if he were a Weeble. Dough-Boy waits on them at breakfast, lunch, and dinner and if he isn't quick enough, "Tashtego had an ungentlemanly way of accelerating him by darting a fork at his back, harpoon-wise." Daggoo and Tashtego also double up torturing the "pale, loaf-of-bread" kid, whose "whole life was one continual lip-quiver."

So that's Team Pequod. Save for one we have yet to meet. He's the captain of the team, the top of the heap, the big kahuna, el jefe, the boss man—the kingfish, if you will, and the guy who merits his very own chapter: "Ahab."

13
CALL HIM AHAB

In which Ishmael learns that Ahab lost a leg to a whale and is still pretty steamed about it

His name is Ahab, of course. Anyone with even a passing knowledge of *Moby Dick* knows that the captain's name is Ahab. His mother named him. "Let's call him Ahab," she said.

And so, the kid was doomed from the start. Read the Bible (The Classics Slacker may not get to it any time soon). The story is right there in Kings: *And so it came to pass that Ahab dideth such evil wickednesses that made the Lord really, really mad.*

Naturally Ishmael, the know-it-all, knows the Bible from "in the beginning" to "the end is near." So back when he was interviewing for the *Pequod* job, and Peleg happened to mention that the captain's name was Ahab, our Ishmael said in short: Wait. What?

Hey, he didn't name himself, said Peleg. "'Twas a foolish ignorant whim of his crazy widowed mother, who died when he was only a twelvemonth old."

Poor Ahab was not only orphaned by a crazy widow, he was orphaned by a crazy widow who stuck him with a stupid name. Ishmael started to feel sorry for his future boss and more comfortable about taking the job. In fact, he was just about to sign on the dotted line when Peleg stopped him. Just one more thing "before ye bind yourself to it past backing out."

Captain Ahab is, well, "kind of moody." Really more like "desperate moody." Okay, if you must know, he's "savage sometimes." But you'd be a little pouty, too, if you only had one leg.

"What do you mean, sir?" asked Ishmael. "Was the other one lost by a whale?"

"Lost by a whale!" cried Peleg. That whale didn't just nibble on Ahab's leg as if it were a cucumber sandwich. "It was devoured, chewed up, crunched by the monstrousest parmacetty that ever chipped a boat!"

But plucky Ahab never let his disability stop him. He simply arranged for his ship to be made handicapped accessible: "Upon each side of the *Pequod*'s quarter deck, and pretty close to the mizzen shrouds, there was an auger hole, bored about half an inch or so, into the plank." So all Ahab had to do was insert end of fake leg into round hole—*et voilà!*—he could steady himself on the deck and look "straight out beyond the ship's ever-pitching prow."

Still, watching him standing there…it's not a pretty picture. "Not a word he spoke; nor did his officers say aught to him; though by all their minutest gestures and expressions, they plainly showed the uneasy, if not painful, consciousness of being under a troubled master-eye. And not only that, but moody stricken Ahab stood before them with a crucifixion in his face; in all the nameless regal overbearing dignity of some mighty woe."

Uneasy, painful…sounds as if everyone is already seasick. Anchors aweigh!

14
SCHOOL OF WHALES

In which "Professor Ishmael" gives a marathon lecture on whales in a soul-crushing chapter called "Cetology"

A third of the way through *Moby Dick,* Melville has a pretty good story going. A couple of guys, of dubious sexuality, are stepping onto a boat with a crazy captain, for what appears to be a long, long time hunting for whales. To the sea, to adventures unknown! To paraphrase Tennyson:

> *Push off, my friends! Let us sail beyond the sunset*
> *It may be that the gulfs will wash us down*
> *Or it may be that we shall kill oodles of whales*
> *And bring home boatloads of blubber*

Or it may be that we remain fully anchored for thirteen pages while Ishmael, who has suddenly morphed from mariner to marine biologist, classifies every whale species that has ever roamed the seas in a chapter called "Cetology."

"It is but well to attend to a matter almost indispensable to a thorough appreciative understanding of the more special leviathanic revelations and allusions of all sorts of which are to follow." He said "almost indispensable," right? Meaning we really could probably follow the story just fine even if we dropped Cetology 101? Besides, what makes Ishmael Mr. Know-It-All Whale Expert?

He isn't, he says, as if anticipating the question. "As no better man advances to take this matter in hand, I hereupon offer my own poor endeavors. What am I that I should essay to hook the nose of this leviathan!" In other words, you are stuck with me, a poor, poor substitute teacher. I beg you to forgive me and to please withhold your firing of spitballs.

Oh, if only Ishmael truly believed himself an unworthy teacher; The Classic Slacker could cut class and throw Frisbees. Instead, Ishmael decides it's okay to impersonate a Ph.D. After all, he has, in his mind at least, equivalent relevant experience. "But I have swam through libraries and sailed through oceans; I have had to do with whales with these visible hands; I am in earnest; and I will try."

That sound you hear is The Classics Slacker searching for a sharp knife with which to gut several personal internal organs. Reading *Moby Dick*—specifically the upcoming "Cetology" chapter—it is a ponderous task! To lay hands upon the unspeakable foundations, ribs, and very pelvis of this book; it is a fearful thing.

But The Classics Slacker slogs on for you, Dear Reader. On the next few pages please accept this poor offering—an abridged version of Ishmael's scientific lecture on whales ("I'll Take Whales for $100, Alex"). It will be faulty, of course. The Classics Slacker is but human and for this reason infallibly faulty. Oh, how one despairs of one's uselessness. Oh, this whole enterprise is but a draught—"nay, but the draught of a draught. Oh, Time, Strength, Cash, and Patience!"

(Feel free to send cash or checks made out to The Classics Slacker.)

THE CLASSICS SLACKER READS MOBY DICK

WHALES	BEGINS WITH "W"	FAMOUS FISH	RHYMES with KALE	MAKES GOOD OIL
$100	$100	$100	$100	$100
$200	$200	$200	$200	$200

15
"I'LL TAKE WHALES FOR $100, ALEX"

In which The Classics Slacker turns the "Cetology" chapter into an enjoyable game

If for some reason you decide to read *Moby Dick* yourself instead of relying on The Classics Slacker to do it for you, it is advised that you grasp the pages of the Cetology chapter and rip them from your copy of the book. For the rest of you, herewith is Ishmael's marine biology lesson reconfigured into a fun game: "Whale Jeopardy!"

The clues and answers, in the form of answers and questions, are already answered (see corresponding numbers). The Classics Slacker would not actually expect anyone to play "Whale Jeopardy!"

42

"I'LL TAKE WHALES FOR $100, ALEX"

And the answers (in the form of questions) are:

1. What is a Sperm Whale?
2. What is a Right Whale?
3. What is a Fin Back Whale?
4. What is a Razor Back Whale?
5. What is a Porpoise?
6. What is a Humpback Whale?
7. What is a Narwhale?

And the clues are:

> THIS "VIVACIOUS" FISH IS "FULL OF FINE SPIRITS" AND "HAILED WITH DELIGHT BY THE MARINER." HE IS CONSIDERED "A LUCKY OMEN," EVOKING "THREE CHEERS" FROM ALL WHO BEHOLD HIM. AFTER YOU STAB HIM TO DEATH, HE PRODUCES A "FINE AND DELICATE" OIL AND HIS "MEAT IS GOOD EATING." (5)

> THIS WHALE'S "GRAND DISTINGUISHING FEATURE" IS OFTEN "A CONSPICUOUS OBJECT." HE IS "VERY SHY," "NOT GREGARIOUS," AND DOES NOT GET ALONG WITH OTHER WHALES. PERHAPS BECAUSE THE OTHER WHALES MAKE FUN OF HIS FIN. (3)

THE CLASSICS SLACKER READS MOBY DICK

"THOUGH NO COWARD," THIS WHALE "HAS NEVER YET SHOWN ANY PART OF HIM BUT HIS BACK, WHICH RISES IN A LARGE SHARP RIDGE." HE HAS EXPERIENCED MANY CLOSE SHAVES. (4)

"THE MOST GAMESOME AND LIGHT-HEARTED OF ALL THE WHALES," HE MAKES "MORE GAY FOAM AND WHITE WATER" THAN ALL THE REST. THAT IS UNTIL "HE IS CAPTURED AND TOWED INTO HARBOR" AND DRAINED OF HIS OIL, WHICH AS IT TURNS OUT, "IS NOT VERY VALUABLE." (6)

THIS WHALE IS NEVER WRONG. OR AT LEAST HE THINKS HE'S ALWAYS RIGHT. WHAT A JERK. (2)

ALSO KNOWN AS THE UNICORN WHALE, THIS WHALE'S "PRODIGIOUS HORN" WAS PRESENTED TO QUEEN BESS BY SIR MARTIN FROBISHER UPON HIS RETURN FROM A VOYAGE. THE EARL OF LEICESTER DID LIKEWISE PRESENT ONE TO HER HIGHNESS. WHICH CAUSED THE QUEEN TO SAY, "GREAT. NOT ANOTHER STUPID HORN." (7)

> THE WHALE FEATURED IN HERMAN MELVILLE'S NOVEL *MOBY DICK*, THE MOST DREADED ASSIGNED READING FOR HIGH SCHOOL STUDENTS SINCE 1852. ALSO NAMED AFTER THE SUBSTANCE LUSTILY DESIRED BY ISHMAEL, QUEEQUEG, AND THE WHOLE LOT OF THEM. (1)

> AND THE FINAL "WHALE JEOPARDY!" CLUE IS: AFTER THE CLASSICS SLACKER SPENT THREE AND A HALF HOURS SUFFERING THOUGH ISHMAEL'S CRUSHINGLY BORING AND EXCEEDINGLY PROTRACTED CETOLOGY DISSERTATION, ONLY TO DISCOVER HIS TEN-WORD ABSTRACT ("A WHALE IS A SPOUTING FISH WITH A HORIZONTAL TAIL"), THE CLASSICS SLACKER WANTED TO COMMIT THIS VIOLENT ACT.

And the answer is: Distill Ishmael's blubber into oil?

Right! That answer qualifies you to go on to the next chapter: "Pole Dancing."

16

POLE DANCING

In which Ishmael takes his first watch on the masthead and discovers he likes getting high

One assumes that Ishmael was hired to do a job of some sort. But thirty-five chapters in, all he does is talk. Finally he's assigned to his first duty—mounting the mast-head. He describes it thusly: "There you stand, a hundred feet above the silent decks, striding along the deep, as if the masts were gigantic stilts, while beneath you and between your legs, as it were *[as it were, indeed]*, swim the hugest monsters of the sea, even as ships once sailed between the boots of the famous Colossus at old Rhodes."

The Classics Slacker is not a gay man. Nonetheless, reading the above passage, one feels a certain, uh, shall we say, stirring in one's…never mind.

The sailors take turns mast-head mounting. They shimmy up the pole and hang out on top for a couple of hours, scanning the water for whales. At least, that's what they're supposed to be doing. Most of the guys enjoy it up there a little too much—when sailing in Southern waters anyway. "In the serene weather of the tropics it is exceedingly pleasant the mast-head: nay, to a dreamy meditative man it is delightful."

Guess who is just such a man? Why our Ishmael, of course, and he doesn't try to hide it, either. "Let me make a clean breast of it here, and frankly admit that I kept but a sorry guard. How could I—being left completely to myself at such a thought-engendering altitude—how could I but lightly hold my obligations to observe all whale-ships' standing orders, 'Keep your weather eye open, and sing out every time.' "

The Classics Slacker imagines the mast-head song goes something like this:

> Do you see what I see?
> Way out in the ocean, there it goes.
> Do you see what I see?
> A whale, a whale, bigger than a kite,
> Let us hope that he doesn't bite.
> Let us hope that he doesn't bite.

But Ishmael doesn't "sing out"; he's a mast-head slacker who'd "rather not see whales than otherwise." And he's not the only one. "Many romantic, melancholy, and absent-minded young men, disgusted with the corking care of the earth" swindle unsuspecting ship-owners into hiring them. Once aboard the ship, they head straight to the mast-head.

Which is a darned good place to be. "The tranced ship indolently rolls; the drowsy trade winds blow; everything resolves you into languor." Even better, you're living off the grid: "You hear no news; read no gazettes; you hear of no domestic afflictions; bankrupt securities; fall of stocks." You don't even have to worry about what to make for dinner because "all your meals for three years and more are snugly stowed in casks, and your bill of fare is immutable."

In modern terms, hanging out on the mast-head is like leaving your cell phone at home and checking into an all-inclusive beach resort—one that excludes women.

But who needs women when whalemen are such excellent pole dancers.

17
BREAKING NEWS

In which Ahab reveals his true motive for the Pequod's *voyage*

Ahab, you may recall, is the captain of the *Pequod*. Thus far, he's been completely harmless. All he does is walk the deck all night, his fake leg click-clacking away. He knows it makes a racket, so he avoids the area where the crew is sleeping just below. "Because to his wearied mates, seeking repose within six inches of his ivory heel, such would have been the reverberating crack and din of that bony step, that their dreams would have been of the crunching teeth of sharks."

What a considerate guy, Ishmael thinks. But his officers know better. They sense that he's about to make a major announcement that will reveal malicious intent. "D'ye mark him, Flask?" whispered Stubb; "the chick that's in him pecks the shell. 'Twill soon be out." Sure enough, Ahab starts peeping; he calls for a meeting of the entire crew.

It starts off with a simple call-and-response. Why are we

here? Ahab bellows. To hunt whales! the crew responds. (Like, duh.) Then Ahab raises the stakes. "Look ye! d'ye see this Spanish ounce of gold?—holding up a broad bright coin to the sun—it is a sixteen dollar piece, men. D'ye see it?"

Yep, they definitely see it. But how to get it? Simple. "Whosoever of ye raises me a white-headed whale with a wrinkled brow and a crooked jaw; whosoever of ye raises me that white-headed whale, with three holes punctured in his starboard fluke—look ye, whosoever of ye raises that same white whale, he shall have this gold ounce, my boys!"

Ahab, you may have noticed, is given to repetition. Just in case there's any confusion, he emphasizes that the whale he wants is white. It's a white whale. White, white, white, white. Whale, whale, whale, whale. Ahab could not be clearer. He wants a white whale. Preferably one that's white.

The crew—idiots to a man—are totally on board with the idea. " 'Aye, aye!' shouted the harpooneers and seamen, running closer to the excited old man: 'A sharp eye for the White Whale; a sharp lance for Moby Dick!' " However, their superior—Starbuck—isn't buying it. That's why he's superior. Starbuck says: "Look, dude *[paraphrasing here]*, if in the course of doing business we happen to kill Moby Dick, that's fine with me. But I didn't come on this trip just to chase a stupid white whale who was mean to you."

He didn't. But he will. Ahab makes him change his mind. Find out how in the next chapter: "Exhale and Inwhale."

18

EXHALE AND INWHALE

In which Ahab uses strange nasal magic to draw reluctant Starbuck over to his side

Ahab continues to rant on and on about finding and killing the White Whale. Nobody on or within earshot of the *Pequod* can escape his constant bellowing—not the officers, harpooneers, sailors, seagulls, clams, oysters, and algae. Even after everyone has already enthusiastically agreed to drop everything and instead focus all their energy on looking for Moby Dick, Ahab just won't shut up about it.

" 'Aye, aye,' he shouted with a terrific, loud, animal sob, like that of a heart-stricken moose; 'Aye, aye! It was that accursed white whale that razeed me; made a poor pegging lubber of me for ever and a day!' "

True, it was an unfortunate series of events. First Ahab was razeedized by the whale, which left him walking around on a two-by-four. Ever since, he's been wailing like Bullwinkle suffering from angina. The guy's a wreck. The whale was a dick. Ahab figures if he fillets the whale, everything will be all right. Makes perfect sense to him.

He had worried about persuading the crew, but in retrospect, he pulled it off without too much trouble. " 'Twas not so hard a task. I thought to find one stubborn, at the least; but my one cogged circle fits into all their various wheels, and they revolve."

All except Starbuck, that is, whose ball bearings squeaked, stuttered, and pulled to the left; he's like a bad wheel on Ahab's grocery store cart.

"Vengeance on a dumb brute!" Starbuck had protested, "that simply smote thee from blindest instinct." In short, he was saying, whales will be whales. Hardly indisputable.

Starbuck might have continued to argue his point were he not infected by a brain-washing substance that emanated from Ahab's nasal passages. Weird, yes, but that's what happened. Reports Ahab: "Something shot from my dilated nostrils, he has inhaled it in his lungs. Starbuck now is mine; cannot oppose me now, without rebellion." Starbuck concurs: "He drilled deep down, and blasted all my reason out of me!"

First mate Starbuck has become a nasal officer. And no amount of Afrin in all the supermarket aisles in all the world can save him.

19
DANCING QUEENS

In which the guys celebrate their plan to kill Moby Dick with a rollickin' party

Baited by Ahab and reeled in like a hapless, hopeless flounder, Starbuck is screwed and he knows it. He sees the "grim, phantom futures" and the "latent horrors" to come. Not so his idiot shipmates. They have pledged allegiance to Ahab and his mission; it's time to celebrate.

What follows is a dance party that—little known fact—served as the inspiration for the Disney ride "It's a Small World." (The Classics Slacker apologizes if that insipid tune remains stuck in your head for days.) You have your Dutch guy, your French guy, your Icelandic guy, your Italian guy, your New York guy (Long Island specifically), your Chinese guy, your Tahitian guy, your Portuguese guy, your English guy, your Spanish guy, your Irish guy, two African-American guys, and three Nantucket guys, who are identified only by numbers. Those are the guys who had terrible auditions.

Stereotypes aplenty. The guy from Iceland is cold, the guy from Holland likes cheese, the Italian lusts after women. And so on.

There's a lot of action here performed by a lot of characters. How to wrangle them into one chapter?

HERMAN MELVILLE: Gosh my hand is tired from writing all these long sentences. *(He puts down his pen and flexes his fingers.)* I know! *(An imaginary light bulb flicks on over his head.)* I'll write the rest of this chapter like a Broadway musical! It will be more successful than *Anything Goes!*

Herewith The Classics Slacker reveals Melville's never-before-seen first draft of chapter 40: "Midnight, Forecastle."

FRENCH SAILOR *(leaping to his feet)*: Hey, *mes frères*! We haf thrown our *chapeaus* into ze ring to merder ze Whale Blanche! But first, we dance! Jig it, men, I say; merry's the word; hurrah! *(They do not move.)* Mon dieu, won't you dance? Come on, baby, do the locomotion! Throw yourselves! Legs! Legs! *(To Pip)* Peep! little Peep! hurrah with your tambourine.

(Pip beats on his tambourine. The sailors commence to dance.)

AZORE SAILOR: Go it, Pip! Bang it, bell-boy! Rig it, stig it, tell me can you dig it, baby?

CHINESE SAILOR: Pound away! Make like a pagoda!

FRENCH SAILOR: Hold up ze hoop, Peep, till I zhump through eet!

MALTESE SAILOR *(looking around with alarm)*: Wait. Is everyone on this ship GAY? I don't want to dance with dudes. *(Gazing dreamily at the ocean)* Would all the waves were women, then I'd go drown and chassee with them evermore! There's naught so sweet on earth—heaven may not match it!—as those swift glances of warm, wild bosoms in the dance, when the over-arboring arms hide such ripe, bursting grapes.

SICILIAN SAILOR *(inspecting his crotch)*: That's a spicy meatball! I love-a to watch-a the womens to danza. Those-a fleet interlacings of the limbs—lithe swayings—coyings—flutterings! lip! heart! hip!

TAHITIAN SAILOR *(writhing on his mat)*: You dudes ain't seen nothing like the holy nakedness of our dancing girls. Heeva-Heeva! Bust my coconuts! I'm with you two. I will not do any man-dancing.

LONG-ISLAND SAILOR *(leering at the men)*: Oh you sulkies, do you see any chicks here? Fuggetaboutit. There's plenty more of us. I sez hoe corn when you may. Cuz one day, we'll all be swimmin' with da fishes. I sez luv da one you're wid.

MALTESE SAILOR: Well, you have a point there.

(All nod their heads and dance with each other.)

DAGGOO *(looking disgusted)*: Man, these white guys are terrible dancers.

ENGLISH SAILOR *(Removing his pipe from his mouth)*: I say, lads, enough with the bloody dancing. Don't let's forget a cheer for our dear Captain Ahab. Blimey, but that old man's a grand old cove! And we are the lot he chose to hunt and harrier him up his whale! *(Sings)* "For he's a jolly good fellow, for he's a jolly good fellow..."

(All raise mugs of ale and join in the singing.)

In due time, everyone is as drunk as sailors and passed out on the deck. As dawn arises, so does our narrator, Ishmael, who, despite a massive hangover, resumes the tale in the next chapter titled, appropriately enough: "Moby Dick."

20
YOU DON'T KNOW DICK

In which Ishmael realizes that he lacks critical information about the White Whale

It's the morning after the big "Let's Get Moby Dick" dance party. Ishmael extricates himself from under a pile of dead-drunk sailors still sleeping it off and starts to consider the situation.

Okay, he says. I don't remember much about last night. But I'm pretty sure that when all the others took oaths of violence and revenge, I, Ishmael, was one of that crew. My shouts had gone up with the rest. But now that I've sobered up, I'm wondering if I just got all caught up in some mob mentality. I don't know the first thing about this white whale that everybody calls Moby Dick.

So Ishmael starts asking around. "With greedy ears I learned the history of that murderous monster." Some are facts; other just "wild rumors."

He's white: "He had gained his distinctive appellation of the

White Whale; a name, indeed, literally justified by his vivid aspect, when seen gliding at high noon through a dark blue sea, leaving a milky-way wake of creamy foam, all spangled with golden gleamings." So pretty!

He's ubiquitous: "He had actually been encountered in opposite latitudes at one and the same instant of time." Like Elvis.

He's big as a whale: A "leviathan" of "uncommon magnitude," "uncommon bulk," and "enormous girth." He would likely break the scale at a Weight Watchers weigh-in.

He's ugly: He has "a peculiar snow-white wrinkled forehead," "a high, pyramidical white hump," and "a deformed lower jaw." A face only his mother, Mrs. Dick, could love.

He has a temper: He possesses "great ferocity, cunning, malice, and direful wrath." If chased, he doesn't just swim away with his tail between his legs. Oh no. "He had several times been known to turn around suddenly, and, bearing down upon his pursuers, either stave their boats to splinters, or drive them back in consternation to their ship."

He's thick-skinned: Even if "groves of spears should be planted in his flanks, he would still swim away unharmed." Names will never hurt him, either.

He does bodily harm: "Such calamities did ensue in these assaults—not restricted to sprained wrists and ankles, broken limbs, or devouring amputations (e.g., Ahab's leg)—but fatal to the last degree of fatality." He left the whalemen not only merely dead, but really most sincerely dead.

Yet more stories emerge, each one nastier than the one before. Ishmael grows increasingly alarmed.

Finally he hears the details of Ahab's encounter with Moby Dick. How Ahab had attacked the White Whale with a "six-inch blade"—not exactly choosing the best tool for the job—and subsequently became "unlimbed of a leg." Adding insult to injury, Moby Dick was especially mean about it. "No turbaned Turk, no hired Venetian or Malay, could have smote him with more seeming malice."

Ishmael has heard enough. And now that he's fully acquainted with Moby Dick's dossier, he would very much like to abandon ship. But that's not gonna happen anytime soon. Not for a least another 300 pages.

21

A WHITER SHADE OF WHALE

In which the only thing more grotesquely white than the White Whale is Mitch McConnell

"What the white whale was to Ahab, has been hinted," says Ishmael. Hinted? Really? That may be the biggest understatement in the history of literature. It would be like saying Romeo was fond of Juliet, and Frankenstein was a tad unattractive.

"What he was to me," says Ishmael, "as yet remains unsaid." True. But not for long. The "as yet unsaid" will be said in the next 25 paragraphs, including one sentence that runs 458 words. No joke. The Classics Slacker counted them for you. You're welcome.

From what Ishmael has heard—and he's heard a lot at this point—he won't care for Moby Dick. It's not so much the whale's size, his ugly mug, or his taste for Ahab-kebobs. No. What terrifies Ishmael the most is Moby Dick's color. Hint: It's white. "It was the whiteness of the whale that above all things appalled me."

Whiteness is the worst part? Ishmael, explain yourself: "But how can I hope to explain myself here, and yet, in some dim, random way, explain myself I must."

His explanation is indeed dim and random. But much like whale blubber, it all boils down to this: To Ishmael, some white things are good, but way more white things are bad.

For example, good white things are pearls and japonicas, bridal gowns and marble. Bad white things are albinos and polar bears. Good white things are horses and lambswool and clerics' robes. Bad white things are dead people and ghosts, fog and flags, shrouds and crosses. Not to mention "the muffled rollings of a milky sea; the bleak rustlings of the festooned frosts of mountains; the desolate shiftings of the windrowed snows of prairies."

And white whales? Bad.

Inspired by Ishmael's discourse on the color white, The Classics Slacker has also come up with a list of good white things and bad white things.

Good White Things:

Cottonelle toilet paper with aloe and vitamin E
Daisies
Doves
Coconut macaroons
Teeth
Philadelphia Cream Cheese
Wite-Out
Clouds
Popcorn
Elmer's Glue-All
Rice pudding
Epsom salts
Snowflakes

Bad White Things:

Slugs
Supremacists
Panties
Really bad: white panties under white pants
Mitch McConnell
The stuff inside Twinkies, Oreos, Ding-Dongs, and Ho-Ho's
Pus
Mitch McConnell (again)
Tofu
Hospital bills
White-nose Syndrome (a disease that afflicts bats and
    Mitch McConnell)
Angel food cake
Rabies
Nazis
Wonder bread
Styrofoam peanuts

So there it is. The Classics Slacker has reached the same conclusion as Ishmael. There are in fact more bad white things than good white things. It's as clear as black and white.

22

AHAB'S MEN-O-PAUSE

Too many months on the ship have elicited symptoms in Ahab that are usually seen only in women over 50

M*oby Dick* is a pretty darn masculine book. Written by a man, narrated by a man, featuring a man and his men who have gone fishin' for an enormous Sperm Whale. The only women so far mentioned are Bildad's sister, Charity, who packs the sailors' lunches ("she would come on board with a jar of pickles") and Mrs. Hosea Hussey, she of the Try Pots Inn who serves Ishmael and Queequeg chowder for breakfast, lunch, and dinner. ("Clam or cod?")

So it's raining men, men, men all over the pages of Melville's novel. But one character, indeed Captain Ahab himself, has distinctly female attributes. He seems just like a woman, especially a postmenopausal one. (Full disclosure here…it takes one to know one.)

First, let's take a look at his face—something most women of a certain age do with increasing alarm. His has more wrinkles than a linen skirt. Moreover, Ahab knows nothing about flattering lighting. He works under a heavy pewter lamp suspended by a chain over his head. "[It] for ever threw shifting gleams and shadows of lines upon his wrinkled brow, till it almost seemed that while he himself was marking out lines and courses on the wrinkled charts, some invisible pencil was also tracing lines and courses upon the deeply marked chart of his forehead."

Ahab, The Classics Slacker has one word for you: Botox. Not only will it fill out your wrinkles, it is purported to alleviate migraine headaches, which you (and 27 million U.S. women) suffer from. Ahab's symptoms include "blazing brain," "insufferable anguish," "clashing phrensies," and a "mad mind." Some migraines are relieved when the patient is exposed to fresh air, which in Ahab's world is plentiful, thank goodness.

The wizened captain is also subject to bouts of insomnia, hot flashes, and night sweats. He goes to bed "long after midnight," missing critical beauty sleep. And when at last he hits the pillow, he doesn't exactly drift off into a restorative slumber. He's up and down all night. Plagued by "exhausting and intolerably vivid dreams," his body overheating with "flames and lightnings," Ahab is forced from his hammock and bursts from his state room, "as though escaping from a bed that was on fire." When he does manage to sleep, it is with "clenched hands; and wakes with his own bloody nails in his palms." (And not a manicurist in sight.)

More evidence of Ahab's latent womanliness: He's as angry as a rejected mistress stuck with a bad perm—like Glenn Close in *Fatal Attraction*. He had a nice pair of gams before Moby Dick spirited one away. Now he can't find a decent pair of jeans that fit. He's out for revenge and will not stop until he gets it. He has studied M.D.'s regular routes and knows the big guy's usual haunts as well—"his casual stopping-places and ocean-inns"—where he likes to kick back with an India Whale Ale.

Ahab will track him down, and when he does, well, The Classics Slacker suspects it will end badly for them both. You never know what might happen when a man goes through menopause.

23
CASE CLOSED

In which Ishmael, arguing for the prosecution, aims to prove that Sperm Whales are mean

Ishmael is at it again. No, not canoodling with Queequeg. Not dancing with the dudes. Not even swinging from the masthead. No. He's arguing a case. He says he must prove, beyond a reasonable doubt, that Moby Dick is a mean-spirited jerk. And not just M.D., but all Sperm Whales. "It is very often observed that, if the Sperm Whale, once struck, is allowed time to rally, he then acts, not so often with blind rage, as with wilful, deliberate designs of destruction to his pursuers."

Heck, can you blame him? The Sperm Whale's life is unfolding just swimmingly when people start attacking him with pointed sticks, intent on killing him and boiling his blubber down into "a peculiarly valuable oil."

The Classics Slacker thinks that pretty much sums up the situation. But not Ishmael. He knows he's gone over all this material before, but it's just not enough, kids. "The leading matter of it requires to be still further and more familiarly enlarged upon, in order to be adequately understood, and moreover to take away any incredulity which a profound ignorance of the entire subject may induce in some minds, as to the natural verity of the main points of the affair."

The Classics Slacker is beyond willing to stipulate all points, be they main or minor. Couldn't we just skip 'em and move on with the story? Assuming there is a story. Because, thus far, more than 200 pages in, nothing of any consequence has happened beyond the bromance of Ishmael and Queequeg.

Apparently Ishmael believes there are alleged doubters out there among the readers who have managed to hang in there this far, the ones he refers to as "some minds." And it is for them that our narrator drones on and on (and on), offering into evidence many mind-numbing citations from scientific whale people.

This chapter is called, appropriately enough, "The Affidavit." In it, Ishmael swears—as if before an unhappy jury desperate to break for lunch—that Sperm Whales really are big ("uncommon large"), and that they really are nasty ("judiciously malicious"). Some are even so infamously dickish as to have earned "ocean-wide renown" complete with WWF-like nicknames. (Think Hulk Hogan, Sea-Man Slaughterer, Mariner the Animal, Debbie "The Fishhook" Johnson.) There's Moby Dick, natch, but also Timor Tom, New Zealand Jack, Morquan, and Don Miguel (a mucho macho pescado).

There's more, much more, sworn testimony from Ishmael, none of which you need to know, trust me. For The Classics Slacker—left hand on the Bible, right hand raised—solemnly swears to have read every last word of chapter 45, and tells you now, you're not missing anything. That's the whole truth and nothing but the truth.

24
RAZZLE-DAZZLE 'EM

In which Ahab, worried that he's oversold the whole Moby Dick thing, pulls regular whales out of his hat

Timing, they say, is everything, and Ahab made a critical blunder when he spilled the beans about his secret goal to slay Moby Dick. Says Ishmael: "He impulsively, it is probable, and perhaps somewhat prematurely revealed the prime but private purpose of the *Pequod*'s voyage." In short, he spoke too soon—and used entirely too many p's.

Sure the "savage crew had hailed the announcement of his quest." But how long would their passion for the pursuit last? Pretty soon they'd be pissed off when they picked up that they'd been played. "Ahab had indirectly laid himself open to the unanswerable charge of usurpation; and with perfect impunity, both moral and legal, his crew if so disposed could refuse all further obedience to him, and even violently wrest from him the command."

Doh! declares Ahab. Did I derail it? Darn! But the deed is done. And with due diligence I must do damage control. Diminish the deception. *(Deeply deliberating)* I divine it! Distract them!

It is doubtful that dames will do it. Besides, there is a dearth of them.

The obvious answer: money. "I will not strip these men of all hopes of cash—aye cash," says Ahab. Before they are onto him, he'll pretend that he cares much more about hunting regular old whales than chasing after Moby Dick. "For even the high lifted and chivalric Crusaders of old times were not content to traverse two thousand miles of land to fight for their holy sepulchre, without committing burglaries, picking pockets, and gaining other pious perquisites by the way. Had they been strictly held to their one final and romantic object, too many would have turned from it in disgust."

While Ahab ponders his position, Ishmael and Queequeg—those two lazy lovebirds—are lounging on the deck weaving mats, "on a cloudy sultry afternoon," with nary a thought of hunting, killing, or cash. When you're in love, who cares about money? Ishmael describes their motions, which sound a lot like…well, you be the judge: "I kept passing and repassing the filling or woof of marline between the long yarns of the warp, using my own hand for the shuttle, and Queequeg, standing sideways, ever and anon slid his heavy oaken sword between the threads."

Their wefting and woofing continues until the threads become "one single, ever returning, unchanging vibration," ending abruptly with a man's cry. It is "a sound so strange, long drawn, and musically wild and unearthly."

The sound, as it turns out, emanates from "that mad Gay-Header, Tashtego," who yells, 'There she blows! there! there! there! she blows! she blows!' "

" 'Where-away?' "

" 'On the lee-beam, about two miles off! a school of them!' "
At long last! We have whales! Let's get 'em!

25

THE MORE THE MERRIER

In which the guys discover that Ahab has squirreled away five extra rowers in his quarters

Tashtego sees whales! Yay! This is the moment the crew (and The Classics Slacker) have been waiting and waiting and waiting for. The sailors spring into action, suddenly busy as elves on Christmas Eve. They jump down from the fore and mizzen, they fix the line tubs in their places, they thrust out the cranes, they back the mainyard, they deck the halls, they slice the fruitcake. All of this must be done in order to release the whaleboats attached to the *Pequod*. It is in those boats that the sailors will row close to the whales—and pounce.

All unfolds according to standard operating procedure when, what to their wondering eyes should appear, but five never-before-seen crew members. Surprise, *Pequod* people. Whales aren't the only mammals that have emerged from the deep. Ahab has been keeping these dudes in his room, presumably hidden in the back of the closet, like suits saved for a special occasion. And now that occasion—"this critical instant"—has arrived. He brings them up to the deck without so much as an "Ahoy, there" and puts them into service as his personal rowers.

These guys have appeared so suddenly that everyone thinks they might be "five phantoms freshly formed out of air." The Pequoders drop everything—from fores to mizzens, cranes to mainyards—and freeze like the doomed citizens of Pompeii.

Ahab shocks them back to life with a "Hey! What's everybody looking at? Get back to work!"

But it's hard not to stare, because the five of them are a hair-raising sight, starting with their captain, Fedallah, whose hair is literally raised. "Strangely crowning this ebonness [dark skin, black "Chinese jacket" with "wide black trowsers"] was a glistening white plaited turban, the living hair braided and coiled round and round upon his head." He doesn't exactly have a winning smile, either. He has "one white tooth evilly protruding from its steel-like lips." Its? Fedallah doesn't even merit a personal possessive pronoun.

Ishmael considers the other four guys even scarier than Fedallah. "Less swart in aspect, the companions of this figure were of that vivid, tiger-yellow complexion peculiar to some of the aboriginal natives of the Manilla—a race notorious for a certain diabolism of subtilty, and by some honest white mariners supposed to be the paid spies and secret confidential agents on the water of the devil."

Okay, so race relations had a ways to go back in 1851.

Anyway, as Ahab stands in his boat like Washington crossing the Delaware, "the five strangers" surround him, rowing like mad. At this point Starbuck and Stubb huddle up and discuss the situation.

"Mr. Starbuck," asks Stubb, "what think ye of those yellow boys, sir!"

"Smuggled on board, somehow, before the ship sailed. A sad business, Mr. Stubb! But never mind, Mr. Stubb, all for the best. There's hogshead of sperm ahead, Mr. Stubb, and that's what ye came for." Mr. Stubb might have also come for someone to help him remember his name.

Mr. Stubb doesn't think these new circumstances are quite so sad. Indeed Mr. Stubb thinks they are a bonus. "They are only five more hands come to help us—never mind from where—the more the merrier."

Now, let's get this party started.

26
JUST SAY ROW

*And say lots of other verbs, too!—and adverbs—
to motivate your oarsmen*

You would be amazed, as was The Classics Slacker, at how many different ways a whaleboat captain can command his crew to row. Why, there are as many words for "row" as Eskimos have for "Wow, it's really cold out here." There are also scores of nicknames for the crew, too. And adverbs that "help" (English teacher lingo) the verbs in case their arms get tired.

Weirdly (adverb intended), in *Moby Dick*, the mates use adverbs that contradict each other. They exhort their crews to row fast, then easy, then strong—sometimes all within the same sentence. The poor rowers must feel like they are playing some sadistic game of "Red Light, Green Light."

The second most-used verb after "row" is "pull." And the most common nickname for the crew is "boys." Thus, "Row, boys!" or "Pull, boys!" would cover it. If you command your crew with either of these exhortations, they will almost certainly grab hold of the oars and move them in unison from front to back, thus driving the boat forward toward the goal of whale.

"But why use two words when you can use twenty!" Melville no doubt said to himself while writing chapter 48, glancing at his shelves full to bursting with ink bottles.

Lucky for you, The Classics Slacker has created a simple row chart (pun of course intended) you can refer to. Using this chart, and without reading *Moby Dick,* you'll learn how whaleboat captains in days of yore coxswained their oarsmen.

Verb (for Row)	Nickname (for Crew)	Adverb (to help)	Punctuation Mark (Mandatory)
Pull	Boys	Strong	!
Stroke	Men	Easy	!
Spring	My Lads	Long and Strong	!
Seethe Her	My Chaps	Softly	!
Start Her	My Fine Hearties	Steadily	!
Give Way	My Children	Truly*	!
Break Your Backbones	My Little Ones	Madly*	!
Crack Your Backbones	My Sucklings	Deeply*	!
Burst All Your Livers and Lungs	My Heroes	Metaphorically*	!
Break Something	You Babes	Painfully*	!
Bite Something	You Dogs	Rabidly*	!
Start Something	My Steel-bits, My Silver-spoons, My Marling-spikes	Metallurgically*	!
Behave*	You Rascals	Immediately*	!
Get a Grip*	Ye Ragamuffins	Deliciously*	!
Wake Up*	Ye Sleepers	Groggily*	!
Sauté*	Ye Rapscallions	Hungrily*	!

(*In truth, these words were not used by whaleboat captains in days of yore. The Classics Slacker added them just to fill out the chart.)

27

ISHMAEL GETS WET

*During Ishmael's first whale hunt,
he catches lots of water but comes up dry*

For the first time into the voyage, the *Pequod* has an opportunity to take down a whale. Or two. Heck, there's a whole school of them just hanging around their lockers. But what starts as a thrilling adventure—"full of quick wonder and awe"—becomes just a big wet disaster. Four boats take up the chase and four boats return—with nary a whale to show for it. Not one whale of any color, much less a white one.

Ishmael is an oarsman on Starbuck's boat. In between strokes, he shoots lusty glances at Ahab's personal detail of five hand-picked rowers. They are outdistancing everyone. "Those tiger yellow creatures of his seemed all steel and whalebone; like five trip-hammers they rose and fell with regular strokes of strength." Fedallah, the head guy, is particularly fetching. "He had thrown aside his black jacket, and displayed his naked chest with the whole part of his body above the gunwale, clearly cut against the alternating depressions of the watery horizon."

Ishmael snaps back to attention when Starbuck entreats his oarsmen to "pull strong, come what will." What comes is nasty weather. Dark clouds form, the wind picks up, and a thick mist enshrouds everything. The other three captains, even nutty Ahab, look at the gathering storm and throw it into reverse. Not so Starbuck. He tells his guys, "There is still time to kill a fish yet before the squall comes."

Starbuck is an idiot. His crew is even dumber for obeying him. Soon they hear "an enormous wallowing sound as of fifty elephants stirring in their litter." Since elephants aren't often found in the ocean, one can only assume the sound is coming from a whale. This is confirmed when Starbuck sees its definitive characteristic. "That's his hump. There, there, give it to him," he commands his harpooneer, Queequeg.

But the "darted iron of Queequeg" may as well have been a bobby pin for all the damage it does. The whale "rolled and tumbled like an earthquake beneath us." If you're sitting in a boat and you've got an earthquake erupting beneath you, you're not going to be sitting for long. Starbuck's crew is "tossed helter-skelter in the white curdling cream of the squall." Meanwhile the whale "merely grazed by the iron, escaped." No doubt sniggering all the way.

The guys—along with their oars, harpoons, and other various and sundry accoutrements—are scattered everywhere. After they swim around retrieving all their stuff, they wait miserably—"wet, drenched, and shivering cold"—for the *Pequod* to rescue them. The storm continues to rage around them. It is dawn by the time the last man—Ishmael—is dragged back onto the deck.

While still wet and "shaking [himself] in [his] jacket to fling off the water," Ishmael asks a few pointed questions.

To Queequeg: "My fine friend, does this sort of thing often happen?"

To Stubb: "Is going plump on a flying whale with your sail set in a foggy squall the height of a whaleman's discretion?"

To Flask: "Is it an unalterable law in this fishery, for an oarsman to break his own back pulling himself back-foremost into death's jaws?"

The answers are yes, yes, and yes.

With that, Ishmael decides to draw up his will.

"Queequeg," said I, "come along, you shall be my lawyer, executor, and legatee."

At least Ishmael has one thing that's still dry—his wit.

28
ONCE UPON A MIDNIGHT DREARY

In which a whole lot of creepy omens begin to appear, including ravens who will nevermore quit the ship

The first disastrous attempt to nab a whale causes the mood on the *Pequod* to sink to new depths. Over days that groan into weeks, the ship sails aimlessly up and down the Atlantic Ocean, past the Azores, the Cape de Verdes, the Rio de la Plata, the House of the Rising Sun. Everybody feels gloomy and really, really cold. Worse, an apparition starts showing up in the water every few nights. Not surprisingly, it looks just like a white whale, and it lures them helplessly forward, like the Ghost of Christmas Future.

The "Spirit-Spout" (the title of chapter 51) first reveals itself on a "serene and moonlight night, when all the waves rolled by like scrolls of silver; and, by their soft, suffusing seethings, made what seemed a silvery silence, not a solitude; on such a silent night a silvery jet was seen." It's a wonder that the whale doesn't drown in the Sea of Alliteration.

It's not all that unusual to see whales at night, explains Ishmael, but "not one whaleman in a hundred would venture a lowering for them." Nonetheless, the Spirit-Spout whale casts a spell over the entire crew, stripping them of common sense, rational thought, and standard practices. Every time it's spotted—at midnight, of course—someone yells, "There she blows!" and the whole gang springs into action. Ahab is the first to shake a wooden leg. He scuttles around the deck, commanding for "t'gallant sails and royals to be set, and every stun sail spread."

But as suddenly as the ghost whale appears, it vanishes just as quickly. And everyone is left standing around looking ridiculous. Clearly they are being played. Not too swiftly, they begin to catch on. "There was a peculiar sense of dread that this flitting apparition [was] treacherously beckoning us on and on, in order that the monster might turn round upon us, and rend us at last in the remotest and most savage seas."

As darkness gives way to dawn, another bad sign appears, not from below this time, but from above: ravens, lots of them. It's as if Edgar Allan Poe himself had let loose his entire aviary. "Every morning, perched on our stays, rows of these birds were seen; and in spite of our hootings, for a long time obstinately clung to the hemp, as though they deemed our ship some drifting uninhabited craft; a thing appointed to isolation, and therefore fit roosting-place for their homeless selves."

Did The Classics Slacker mention that it's cold? How cold is it? So cold that one night Starbuck discovers Ahab frozen to his chair like a tongue stuck to a light post in winter. Starbuck had gone to Ahab's cabin "to mark how the barometer stood." And there was the captain "with closed eyes sitting straight in his floor-screwed chair; the rain and half-melted sleet of the storm from which he had some time before emerged still slowly dripping from the unremoved hat and coat."

So it's all around not a jolly time. Between ghost whales, ravens, and cold, the Pequoders are spooked, stalked, and shivering. They could use a good omen. Finally one appears, a fellow whaleship called, appropriately enough, the *Albatross*. Assuming no one shoots it, everything should turn out just fine.

29
LIKE SHIPS PASSING

In which the guys lose the chance to party with sailors from another ship because Ahab is a big ol' wet blanket

If you've been stuck on a whaling ship for 80 million nautical miles with the same guys, telling the same stories, making the same jokes, and exchanging the same furtive glances, the sight of a new ship with different guys with different stories, jokes, and bodies would gladden the hearts and arouse the pituitary glands of just about everyone. Except for Captain Ahab, of course, who has just one thing on his mind, and by now we all know what that one thing is.

The ship's name is the *Albatross* (aka the *Goney*) and she rates—using the Trump classification system—a four at best. She's all at once pale, skinny, and fat. "This craft was bleached like the skeleton of a stranded walrus," describes Ishmael. Ouch! Talk about body image issues. And there's no hiding her age, either. "All down her sides, this spectral appearance was traced with long channels of reddened rust, while all her spars and her rigging were like the thick branches of trees furred over with hoar-frost."

The *Albatross* guys, to the dismay of the *Pequod* squad, are even uglier than their ship. Long in the tooth and even longer in beard, the "forlorn-looking fishermen" seemed "clad in skins of beasts, so torn and bepatched the raiment that had survived nearly four years of cruising."

Still, you take what you can get. So Ishmael gets all excited about the incipient "gam" that will take place between the two ships. Does anyone give a damn what a gam is? Of course not. But our Ishmael, as per usual, begins a dissertation on the subject that begins much like a seventh-grader's book report: "Webster's dictionary describes a 'gam' as…"

Aw, snap! Webster's doesn't *have* a definition for gam, Ishmael scoffs, even though "this same expressive word has now for many years been in constant use among some fifteen thousand true born Yankees."

Ishmael is such an insufferable egghead. "Certainly, it needs a definition," he says, "and should be incorporated into the Lexicon. With that view, let me learnedly define it." So he does, and in a style such that if perchance Noah Webster should happen to swim by, he could just copy and paste it into his deficient dictionary.

"GAM. NOUN—A social meeting of two (or more) Whaleships, generally on a cruising ground; when, after exchanging hails, they exchange visits by boats' crew, the two captains remaining for the time, on board of one ship, and the two chief mates on the other."

A gam can be a brief but intimate meeting of just the top dogs (sniffing each others' butts) or a longer affair with the entire crew (a singles mixer).

However, when the *Pequod* and the *Albatross* draw near each other, hopes for a gam of any kind are quashed faster than you can say "wham gam, thank you, ma'am."

Why? Because Captain Ahab has just one question for the captain of the *Albatross*. You guessed it: "Have you seen the White Whale?"

The *Albatross* captain (we never learn his name) can't even manage a simple yes or no, as weird stuff starts happening "at the first mere mention of the White Whale's name to another ship."

When the "strange captain" leans over the edge of his ship to speak into his trumpet (megaphones hadn't been invented yet), "it somehow fell from his hand into the sea; and the wind now rising amain, he in vain strove to make himself heard without it."

Then all these cute little fishes that had been merrily swimming alongside the *Pequod* freak out. "They darted away with what seemed shuddering fins, and ranged themselves fore and aft with the stranger's flanks." Meaning they quit the *Pequod* and swam to the *Albatross*. They aren't going to wait around for crazy Ahab to turn them into filet o' fishes.

Ahab does not fail to notice their mass exodus. "Swim away from me, do ye?" he says. Indeed they do. Ishmael and the boys would be wise to do the same. Unfortunately they don't have fish for brains.

30

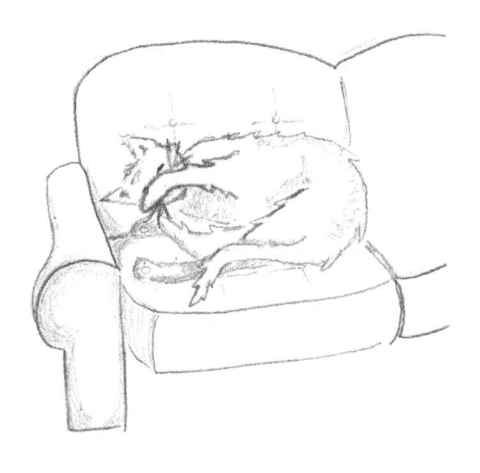

THE TOWN-HO'S STORY

In which The Classics Slacker's cat, Señor Don Gato, braces himself to hear a long tale

The Classics Slacker had long looked forward to reading chapter 55. Its title held such promise: "The Town-Ho's Story." No doubt there would be some titillating tales there, and of the female variety for a change. Perhaps the *Pequod* would make a port of call, and a few of the very few heterosexual crew members would acquaint themselves with an amiable lady of the evening who, in addition to offering her services in exchange for a few pieces of silver, would regale the guys with memorable accounts of her amorous adventures.

Except that, well, no. In *Moby Dick*, the "Town-Ho" is not, as defined in the Urban Dictionary, "the only well-known prostitute in a small town; usually has a friendly personality and clients throughout the community." The *Town-Ho* is a ship. "She" is the second one encountered by the *Pequod*.

The Classics Slacker, though deeply disappointed, nonetheless prepared to bear up against Ishmael's usual style of reportage with its all-too-familiar meanderings. Ishmael promises to make the story extra spicy by telling it as he once did in Lima, of all places, "to a lounging circle of my Spanish friends, one saint's eve, smoking upon the thick-gilt tiled piazza of the Golden Inn."

His friends—among them the "fine cavaliers" Don Pedro and Don Sebastian—must've been smoking something seriously mind-altering to sit around while Ishmael recited a tale that begins: "Some two years prior to my first learning the events which I am about rehearsing to you, gentlemen, the *Town-Ho*, Sperm Whaler of Nantucket, was cruising in your Pacific here, not very many days' sail westward from the eaves of this good Golden Inn." Sober, those guys would've smothered him with a Peruvian serape.

Anyway, what follows is a concise summary of Ishmael's recitation of the *Town-Ho*'s story as once told to The Classics Slacker's slacker cat—Señor Don Gato—as he napped on the finely tufted cushions of the living room sofa. Although most faithfully and briefly rendered, the *Town-Ho*'s story failed to rouse him from his snoozing.

As you might imagine, it's a long, long story, even in brief. It's so long that The Classics Slacker has covered "The *Town-Ho's* Story" in three parts: "Ho"; "Ho, Ho"; and "Ho, Ho, Ho."

31
HO

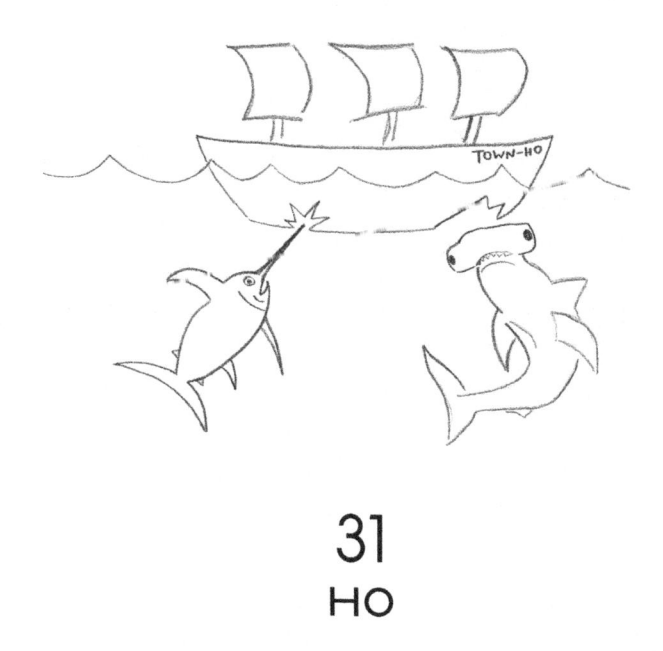

In which the bottom of the Town-Ho *is being damaged by a toolbox full of sea creatures*

The *Town-Ho*'s story was told to the harpooneer Tashtego by three "confederate white seamen" who then swore him to secrecy. But Tashtego babbled part of the story in his sleep and Ishmael shook him down for the rest. Later, much later, Ishmael recites the *Town-Ho*'s story verbatim to a bunch of Dons in Lima. That Ishmael can retell the story word-for-word from Tashtego's dream strains credulity, but so does the idea that the Dons in Lima can stay awake for it.

Don't be surprised if you start nodding off as well. As noted previously, the *Town-Ho*'s story is a long, long, long, really long, story, but The Classics Slacker will try to maintain your interest with this abridged version.

All you really need to know is that the *Town-Ho* encounters Moby Dick, who you may recall is the White Whale. But that detail "never reached the ears of Captain Ahab." Which is a good thing indeed, because if Ahab had heard such news, he would've sent the Pequoders tearing after the White Whale faster than paparazzi chasing Taylor Swift. Anyway, here is the story:

Once upon a time, there were two whalemen on the *Town-Ho*. One of them was "a tall and noble animal with a head like a Roman, and a flowing golden beard like the tasseled housings of your last viceroy's snorting charger; and a brain, and a heart, and a soul in him." His name was Steelkilt and he was a Lakeman, meaning he learned how to sail on the Great Lakes (makes sense). The other, Radney, was the first mate, who hailed from Nantucket. He was "ugly as a mule; yet as hardy, as stubborn, as malicious."

These two had a huge fight and guess who won? A man outfitted in kilt made of steel or a wimp named Radney? But let's not get ahead of ourselves. Melville would surely disapprove.

The *Town-Ho* had enjoyed months of smooth sailing when water started bubbling up onto the floor. The crew determined that the leak must've been caused by a swordfish (possibly working alongside a hammerhead). The only way to fix it would be to head back to the nearest port, drop anchor, and get it patched up. But co-owner Radney, too cheap and greedy to turn the boat around, instead assigned Steelkilt and his team of brawny dudes to pump out the water and keep pumping indefinitely. Which Steelkilt did quite cheerily—the job was appropriate to his manly manliness.

But then Steelkilt teased Radney in front of everyone. "The fact is, boys, that sword-fish only began the job; he's come back again with a gang of ship-carpenters, saw-fish, and file-fish, and what not; and the whole posse of 'em are now hard at work cutting and slashing at the bottom; making improvements, I suppose. If old Rad were here now *[which of course he is]*, I'd tell him to jump overboard and scatter 'em. They're playing the devil with his estate, I can tell him. But he's a simple old soul,—Rad, and a beauty too. Boys, they say the rest of his property is invested in looking-glasses. I wonder if he'd give a poor devil like me the model of his nose."

Radney retaliates by ordering Steelkilt to get a shovel and "remove some offensive matters consequent upon allowing a pig to run at large." It was common knowledge that picking up pig poop was a menial job, one that would never be assigned to "the most athletic seaman of them all" and one who "had been regularly assigned captain of one of the gangs." Radney knew what he was doing: "The order about the shovel was almost as plainly meant to sting and insult Steelkilt, as though Radney had spat in his face."

Nonetheless, Steelkilt was a good-humored pacifist, not given to violence, and so he chuckled to himself and walked away. And they all lived happily ever after. The End.

Ha! If only. The Classics Slacker's coverage of "The *Town-Ho*'s Story" continues in "Ho, Ho."

32
HO, HO

In which first mate Radney scuffles with top-ranked seaman Steelkilt and then everyone piles on

At the end of "Ho" (part 1 of "The *Town-Ho's* Story"), brawny Steelkilt was about to clock wussy Radney, who had stupidly threatened him with a hammer. "Steelkilt told his persecutor that if the hammer but grazed his cheek he (Steelkilt) would murder him."

Guess what happened? "Immediately the hammer touched the cheek; the next instant the lower jaw of the mate was stove in his head; he fell on the hatch spouting blood like *[you got it]* a whale."

Then like a Red Sox-Yankees bench-clearing brawl, "a twisted turmoil ensued" with all the sailors piling on, including a couple of Canallers who "rushed into the uproar."

Exciting stuff, eh? (Even The Classics Slacker's slacker cat, Señor Don Gato, started twitching his ears.) But despite the rising

action of the story, one of Ishmael's listeners, Don Pedro, tragically asks for more details about "Canallers." To which Ishmael replies, "Well then, Don, refill my cup. Your chicha's very fine; and ere proceeding further I will tell ye what our Canallers are; for such information may throw side-light upon my story."
No! No! No! It won't! Canallers are just guys who work on the Erie Canal! Enough said! Too late. Ishmael is already well into yet another digression of the *Town-Ho's* story, babbling on for five pages about Canallers, during which time Señor Don Gato dozed off again.
Don Pedro's eyelids are drooping, too. He sincerely regrets querying Ishmael about Canallers. He begs Ishmael to return to the story, "spilling his chicha upon his silvery ruffles." (Ack! Wine stains on metallic fabric! He'll never get that out.)
Oh yeah right, says Ishmael. Where was I? Ah yes, the *Town-Ho's* story.
Steelkilt and his fellow insurgents barricaded themselves behind some casks. At that point the *Town-Ho's* captain appeared on the scene. With a pistol in each hand the captain roared: "Come out of that, ye cut-throats!"
Steelkilt decided it was time to negotiate. They would go back to work if the captain promised not to punish them. Replied the captain: "Turn to! I make no promises, turn to, I say!" Steelkilt pleaded his case four more times—mostly of the "he started it" variety—but to no avail.
The captain issued an ultimatum: back to work or down into the forecastle—"a place as black as the bowels of despair." Steelkilt chose the latter and convinced the rest of his buddies to do the same.
Long about day four, a few guys started to crack. "The fetid closeness of the air" (putting it delicately), and a "famishing diet" of "water and a couple handfuls of biscuits" (no, not gluten!) did them in. By the fifth day everyone had bailed except for Steelkilt

and the two aforementioned Canallers.

The next day the three holdouts hatched an escape plan. But the Canallers double-crossed Steelkilt. While he was sleeping, they sprang on him. They tied him up and forced him to the deck, offering him up to the captain and presumably saving themselves.

Didn't work. The captain punished the Canallers anyway, flogging them with a rope "till they yelled no more, but lifelessly hung their heads sideways, as the two crucified thieves are drawn." Then Radney, still recovering from his jaw injury, took over, and whipped Steelkilt with the same rope.

Over the next several days, Steelkilt pretended to be chastened. But in fact, he was planning "his own proper and private revenge upon the man who had stung him in the ventricles of his heart." His plan: Wait until Radney is sleeping, then bash in his head with an iron ball. Not too elegant, but effective.

As it turned out, Steelkilt didn't have to murder anybody. "For by a mysterious fatality, Heaven itself seemed to step in to take out of his hands into its own the damning thing he would have done." What did Heaven do? See the third and final installment of the *Town-Ho*'s story: "Ho, Ho, Ho."

33
HO, HO, HO

In which Steelkilt and Ishmael chat over a cup of coffee

At last we have reached the ending of the *Town-Ho*'s story, as told by Ishmael to a bunch of now very drunk Peruvians. To review, Radney had committed three increasingly egregious offenses against Steelkilt: ordered him to scoop pig poop, threatened him with a hammer, and flogged him with a rope. So Steelkilt plots his revenge: He will wait until Radney is asleep and then club him to death like a baby seal.

But who should show up to save him the trouble? Why it's Moby Dick! The White Whale himself, in his debut appearance. One day he is spotted just fifty yards from the *Town-Ho*, and everyone goes all atwitter, like girls at a Beyoncé concert. " 'The White Whale—the White Whale!' was the cry from captain, mates, and harpooneers, who, undeterred by fearful rumours, were all anxious to capture so famous and precious a fish."

The whaleboats were lowered and the men launched their

attack. Radney's boat reached Moby Dick first. And with lance in hand Radney's "bandaged cry was to beach him on the whale's topmost back." But as soon as Radney was hauled up, as per his instructions, he slid right off the whale's "slippery back." (Of course the whale's back was slippery, what else did he expect?) Radney was "tossed over into the sea" and Moby Dick ate him. Or as Ishmael put it: "The whale seized the swimmer between his jaws; and rearing high up with him, plunged headlong again, and went down."

No more Radney. Problem solved.

The rest of the *Town-Ho*'s story is pretty boring actually. It's hard to top a guy being swallowed in one piece like a sushi roll. The ship sailed on, eventually reaching an island "where no civilized creature resided." There most of the crew, headed up by Steelkilt, deserted the *Town-Ho*, stole a double war-canoe from the island's "savages," sailed to Tahiti, and got jobs on a ship headed for France. The end.

But Ishmael's Peruvian friends are skeptical. They think he may have just told 'em a big ol' fish tale. "Did you get it from an unquestionable source?" demands Don Sebastian. Ishmael swears "so help me in Heaven" that he did. "I trod the ship; I knew the crew; I have seen and talked with Steelkilt since the death of Radney."

(It is a Saturday morning at the Nantucket Planet Fitness. Ishmael walks in just as Steelkilt is leaving.)

ISHMAEL: Hey Steely, you ol' seadog! How've you been?
STEELKILT: Um, I'm sorry, who are you?
ISHMAEL: Call me Ishmael.
STEELKILT: Oh right, now I remember.
ISHMAEL: What have you been up to?
STEELKILT: Eh, not much. Pumping iron. A little fishing. You?

ISHMAEL: I spend the majority of my time endeavoring to classify every whale by its Latin nomenclature.

STEELKILT: I see. *(Yawns.)* Hey, who was that guy you used to be with? Quee-something? Are you two still dating?

ISHMAEL: Er, we were just friends. Anyway, he drowned.

STEELKILT: Oh, I'm sorry.

ISHMAEL: Eh, whatever. There are other fish in the sea. Weren't you into some guy named Radney?

STEELKILT: That jerk? We had a huge fight and then he got eaten by Moby Dick.

ISHMAEL: Yipes! Another one bites the dust.

STEELKILT: It's a great story. Let's go to Starbucks and I'll tell you all about it.

34
"BUT I DIGRESS"

In which Ishmael goes off course yet again, treading among even more irrelevant subjects

The Classics Slacker gets a sinking feeling whenever Ishmael strays from the plot and drops anchor, settling on whatever subject he feels like gassing on about for hours and hours. His digressions usually begin with "The tale would be lost if I didn't mention…" or "You would be really confused if I didn't first explain…" or "Let me show off how much I know about _____.

Moby Dick is liberally sprinkled with whole chapters of this nature, covering subjects such as:

Whale Art. A treatise on the pictures, drawings, paintings, sculptures, and figurines of whales as rendered in various mediums. Good information for the next time you're browsing flea markets in Greenland.

Brit. Yellow stuff that floats on the water. Whales eat it when they aren't eating sailors.

The Line. Rope used to snare whales. Either made of hemp ("a dusky dark fellow, a sort of Indian") or Manilla ("a golden-haired Circassian to behold"). Yes, even rope can get Ishmael all man-excited.

The Dart. Heavy implement used to fling into a whale. Could it be yet another of Melville's not-so-subtle symbols of male genitalia? You betcha.

The Crotch. Not what you think. But given all that has come before, you can hardly be blamed.

The Whale as Dish. Delicious vittles to delight everyone at your dining room table.

Whale fritters. "Brown and crisp and smelling something like old Amsterdam housewives' dough-nuts, when fresh." One wonders what they smell like when stale. And when was Ishmael sniffing around old housewives? Before he met Queequeg? Did he try any of their other pastries? This description of whale fritters raises more questions than yeast.

Whale tongue. "A great delicacy in France." Right up there with snails and frog's legs. *Sacre bleech.*

Whale brains. "Two whitish lobes, precisely resembling two large puddings, mixed with flour and cooked." A great delicacy in England, one assumes.

Whale blubber strips. "Exceedingly juicy and nourishing for infants." For when the baby aisle is fresh out of Gerber's puréed liver and beets.

Cutting In. Exactly what it sounds like. Spare you the gory (literally) details.

The Blanket. The skin of a whale. Keeps him warm and cozy. But not so much after he's dead.

The Great Heidelburg Tun. "A wine cask with a capacity of 49,000 gallons." Why wine? Why Heidelburg? Good questions, *meinen liebchen.* The German tun refers to the tun (head) of the

Sperm Whale, which "contains the most precious of his oily vintages." Probably best not to serve it with dinner. Unless you're eating schnitzel with noodles.

Finally Ishmael returns to the main story of Ahab and the guys pursuing Moby Dick. They experience a few hits and misses along the way, as you will discover in the next chapter, "The Subplots Thicken."

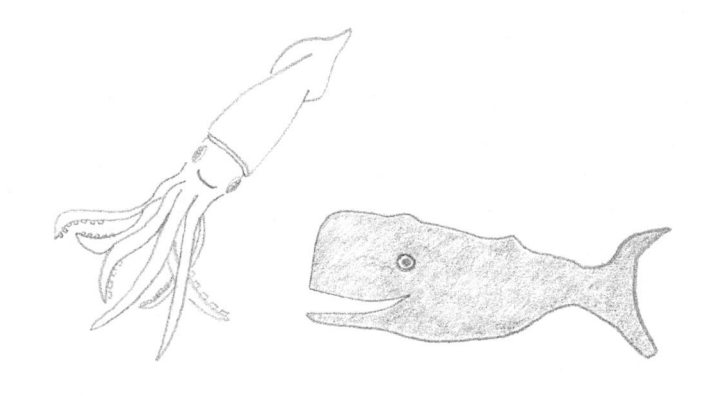

35
THE SUBPLOTS THICKEN

*In which Stubb kills a whale all his own,
and Queequeg prepares to die*

In the second half of *Moby Dick*, The Classics Slacker is sensing (ever so slightly), and hoping (ever so dimly), that the novel may be creeping toward the climactic meeting of man versus fish. But alas, Melville pulls his hapless reader along, as if by vicious undertow, through various detours and subplots. Two in particular take up the most pages: Stubb kills a not-Moby-Dick whale and Queequeg makes funeral arrangements.

Subplot One: Stubb vs. Whale

A giant squid shows up alongside the *Pequod*. The sailors think it might be Moby Dick. It isn't. Although it is "a vast pulpy mass, furlongs in length and breadth, of a glancing cream-color," it disqualifies itself as a whale owing to its "innumerable long arms radiating from its centre, and curling and twisting like a nest of anacondas." Moby Dick is a lot of things, but he ain't a squid.

Nonetheless, the presence of the squid indicates that a Sperm Whale might be frolicking nearby. "When you see him 'quid, then you quick see him 'parm whale." The s-impaired speaker of this observation is Queequeg. A Sparm, er Sperm, Whale is indeed soon spotted, totally minding its own business. He has "a broad, glossy back, of an Ethiopian hue *[in other words, not white]*, glistening in the sun's rays like a mirror, lazily undulating in the trough of the sea, and ever and anon tranquilly spouting his vapory jet." Oh! What an awesome display of nature's beauty! A miracle to behold, really. Why would anyone want to kill… aaaghhh!!!

Stubb flings "dart after dart" and various other sharp objects into the black whale. "His tormented body rolled not in brine, but horribly wallowed in his blood." A prolonged death scene continues for several pages until finally "gush after gush of clotted red gore shot into the frighted air; and falling back again, ran dripping down his motionless flanks into the sea." Nasty.

Before the whale is boiled down for oil, Stubb requests that the ship's cook prepare him a steak dinner, as is the right of the mate who first spots and summarily smites a whale. Dinner is followed by a breakfast of whale balls. Yes, whale balls. No joke.

Stubb does not dine alone. "Mingling their mumblings with his own mastications, thousands on thousands of sharks, swarming round the dead leviathan, smackingly feasted on its fatness." You can see them "wallowing in the sullen, black waters, and turning over on their backs as they scooped out huge globular pieces of the whale of the bigness of a human head." So incredibly gross. Not to mention three successive prepositional phrases in that last sentence.

The whale's body is cut to pieces, boiled, and what's left of

THE SUBPLOTS THICKEN

him is released to sea in a chapter called "The Funeral." It begins with a brief invocation: "Haul in the chains! Let the carcase go astern!" And then, "the peeled white body of the beheaded whale flashes like a marble sepulcher and floats away ever so slowly." Really slowly. "For hours and hours from the almost stationary ship that hideous sight is seen." More hideous still is the leftover head, which is still attached to the *Pequod.*

Ahab chats with the head of Stubb's dead whale. Needless to say, it's a one-way conversation.

Subplot Two: Queequeg vs. Grim Reaper

While pulling up buckets of sperm from the whale's massive head, Tashtego falls in and nearly drowns. Ishmael thinks this would have been a great way to go. "Had Tashtego perished in that head, it had been a very precious perishing; smothered in the very whitest and daintiest of fragrant spermaceti; coffined, hearsed, and tombed in the secret inner chamber and sanctum sanctorum of the whale."

But unfortunately for Tash (as the guys affectionately call him), Queequeg jumps in to save him. Witnessing this selfless act of derring-do, Ishmael is once again besotted by "my brave Queequeg."

Sadly though, by saving Tash, Queequeg might have killed himself. He starts to feel sick, made worse by resuming his nasty job of storing caskets in the hatchway where he must crawl around "amid that dampness and slime." It would be another hundred years before the invention of Tilex Mold & Mildew Remover.

Laments Ishmael: "My poor pagan companion, and fast bosom-friend, Queequeg, was seized with a fever, which brought him nigh to his endless end." Queequeg continues to waste away in his hammock "till there seemed but little left of him but his frame and tattooing." To Ishmael's horror and dismay, the Q-man decides that the end is near and considers how to dispose of his remains.

The "usual sea-custom" is to wrap the dead body in its hammock, burrito-style, and toss it overboard like fish food to the "death-devouring sharks." Queequeg shudders at the thought, and really, who can blame him? He wants a proper coffin and hires the ship's carpenter to build him one. "No sooner was the carpenter apprised of the order, than taking his rule, he forthwith with all the indifferent promptitude of his character, proceeded into the forecastle and took Queequeg's measure with great accuracy." Too bad Double Q was about to breathe his last; with those measurements, the ship's tailor could've fashioned him a tuxedo worthy of the red carpet.

Incidentally, the ship's carpenter doesn't have a proper name; everyone just calls him Carpenter. (More about the carpenter in "If I Were a Carpenter" on page 112.)

When the coffin is finished and carved and polished, Queequeg takes it for a spin and declares it just right for his trip to Eternity. " 'Ah! poor fellow! he'll have to die now,' ejaculated the Long Island sailor." That comment, like a two-paddled defibrillator, shocks Queequeg back to life. Or perhaps the Long Islander's ejaculation roused him. In any case, he starts to feel a lot better. "In good time my Queequeg gained strength; and at length after sitting on the windlass for a few indolent days (but eating with a vigorous appetite) he suddenly leaped to his feet, threw out his arms and legs, gave himself a good stretching, yawned a little bit, and then springing into the head of the hoisted boat, and poising a harpoon, pronounced himself fit to squeeze some sperm."

Kidding! The preceding quote actually ends "pronounced himself fit for a fight." But The Classics Slacker, who by now has become quite the Melville scholar, believes that "squeeze some sperm" appeared in the original text until Melville's homophobic editor changed it.

Still, the writer must've won more than a few editorial battles, as *Moby Dick* fairly drips with "Sperm! Sperm! Sperm!"

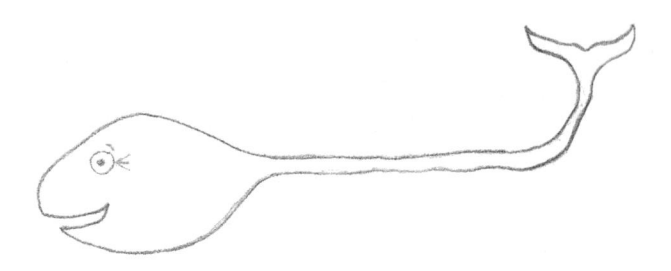

36
SPERM! SPERM! SPERM!

To get a lot of sperm oil, you've got to squeeze a lot of sperm, and the guys are eager to do it

Okay, so the sperm of a Sperm Whale isn't really sperm sperm. It's not the kind of sperm that makes baby whales, and it doesn't produce paroxysms of ecstasy upon exiting the body of the whale. The sperm of a Sperm Whale is stored in its ginormous head, not in his man parts, and that makes a vas deferens.

And yet—and this is the important part—the sperm of a Sperm Whale looks like sperm and feels like sperm and probably tastes like sperm, and Ishmael and the guys just love it!

Fortunately for them, the Sperm Whale has lots and lots of sperm. Tubs of sperm. Roman-bath-sized tubs of sperm. Whale sperm is the substance that gets turned into oil, which is, ostensibly, the whole reason for the trip. To begin the alchemy, the guys have to squeeze the sperm's "soft, gentle globules" for hours. That gives them a perfect excuse for slathering the unctuous goop all

SPERM! SPERM! SPERM!

over themselves and each other all day long. "Squeeze! squeeze! squeeze!" Ishmael rhapsodizes. "I squeezed that sperm till I myself almost melted into it; I squeezed that sperm till a strange sort of insanity came over me." It's called getting aroused, Ishmael. Or did you miss that class in sex ed? "I found myself unwittingly squeezing my co-laborers' hands in it, mistaking their hands for the gentle globules." Oh right, you didn't realize what you were doing? When you're reported to Human Resources, see if they believe you.

Not surprisingly, the scene grows ever hotter and heavier, as Ishmael leads his "co-laborers" into a full-on orgy. "Come; let us squeeze hands all around; nay, let us squeeze ourselves into each other; let us squeeze ourselves universally into the very milk and sperm of kindness." See, it's not just sex—it's love. Aww.

Afterward, Ishmael turns over, sighs deeply, and falls dead asleep (oh, just like a man, no cuddling) and sees in his dreams "long rows of angels in paradise, each with his hands in a jar of spermaceti." Note that the angels of his dreams have man hands.

When Ishmael wakes up in the next chapter, still smiling from his homoerotic "visions of the night," he describes rather coyly, "a very strange enigmatical object" lying lengthwise on the deck. It has been chopped off the Sperm Whale during the "post-mortemizing" process. This object, "an unaccountable cone" is "longer than a Kentuckian is tall, nigh a foot in diameter at its base, and jet-black as Yojo, the ebony idol of Queequeg. And an idol indeed it is." Oh, what could it be? Ishmael teases.

It's a whale penis, people! A penis so big it requires three guys to carry it. One of them, "the mincer" as he is called, "proceeds cylindrically to remove its dark pelt, as an African hunter the pelt of a boa." Then he turns the pelt inside out ("like a pantaloon leg"), cuts a couple of slits for armholes and slips it on like a Halloween costume. ("This year, I'm going as a whale penis.") Dressed as so, he's ready for work, chopping up flesh like so many

105

Vienna sausages.

So, to summarize, the crew bathe themselves in whale sperm and one lucky guy literally wears the skin of its penis like a Slanket. If there is any doubt, any doubt whatsoever, that Ishmael is gay, Queequeg is gay, the whole lot of them are gay, gay, gay, the chapters "A Squeeze of the Hand" and "The Cassock" should lay those doubts to rest. Sadly, tolerance for homosexuality had a long, long way to go from 1851 to 2015 when the Supreme Court legalized same-sex marriage. But at least, in the meantime, the closeted gay community in New England could enjoy a nice, juicy book for their bedtime reading.

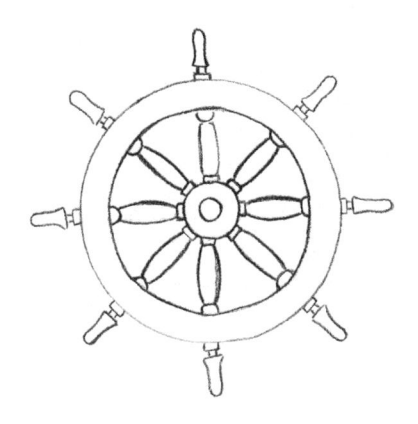

37
FISH AND SHIPS

The sea is full of other whaleships besides the Pequod.
Some are successful; others not so much

It's a big sea. There are lots of fish in there. Our Ahab is looking for just one. Surely someone has seen it, right? Every time the *Pequod* encounters another whaling ship, Ahab asks her captain the same tired question: "Hast seen the White Whale?" Sometimes the answer is "yes," sometimes "no," and sometimes it's "what White Whale?" (They hadn't read the book yet.)

The *Pequod* meets up with nine ships during the course of her voyage. Let's look at them in order of appearance.

THE ALBATROSS
Her status: Rusty.
Her crew: Sunburned.
Her story: Four years of aimless drifting.
Hast seen the WW? Negative.

THE TOWN-HO
Her status: Leaky.
Her crew: Mutinous.
Her story: Way too long. (But if you must know, see "The *Town-Ho's* Story" on page 85.)
Hast seen the WW? Once. Not only did she see Moby Dick, her first mate became M.D.'s lunch.

THE JEROBOAM
Her status: Infected by plague.
Her crew: Soon to be as sick as passengers on a Carnival cruise.
Her story: A schizophrenic sailor has usurped the ship, claiming to be the archangel Gabriel. He seemed right as rain when he was hired, but shortly after pushoff "his insanity broke out in a freshet." The crew made plans to ditch him, but he threatened them with "unconditional perdition" if they did. Weirdly, they believed him. He even claimed to have brought forth the plague and thus could decide who would die and when. The "ignorant crew" believed that, too.
Hast seen the WW? Indeed. Moby Dick flung the *Jeroboam*'s chief mate "bodily into the air" and the "luckless mate fell into the sea at a distance of about fifty yards and for ever sank." Captain Ahab should've taken this tale as a cautionary one, but he's crazier than Gabriel.

THE VIRGIN
Her status: Dark. (All their lamps have run out of oil.)
Her crew: Surprisingly inefficient Germans.
Her story: Hunted for whales but couldn't catch a break, or a whale for that matter. Holding an empty oil can, the dejected Captain Derick De Deer boards the *Pequod* "a-begging" for a refill, just enough to turn on the lights.

Hast seen the WW? *Nein.* Nor a whale of any other color, either.

THE ROSE-BUD
Her status: Weighted down by two decomposing, noxious whales.
Her crew: Fashionably dressed and snooty. They wear "tasseled caps of red worsted" and their noses are "upwardly projected." You guessed it—French. Although in fairness, they are sticking up their noses to avoid breathing in the stench and with it, flesh-eating bacteria.
Her story: Newbie captain hauled in whales that were already dead, which makes them extra smelly and useless for extracting oil. But the captain, "a conceited ignoramus," orders the crew to start cutting up the whales anyway. Sympathetic Stubb figures out a way to liberate the French crew from their "unsavory and unprofitable pickle." Stubb will "advise" the captain in English and a bilingual sailor will fake translate it to the captain, *comme ça:*
STUBB: Tell him that he is no more fit to command a whaleship than a St. Jago monkey. In fact, tell him he's a baboon.
FRENCH SAILOR *(to the captain):* "Monsieur, he conjures us, as we value our lives, to cut loose from these fish."
Et voilà. Problem solved.
Hast seen the WW? *Non.*

THE SAMUEL ENDERBY
Her status: Commanded by a one-armed captain named Boomer.
Her crew: English.
Her story: The ship happened upon a pod of whales. Moby Dick was among them. Captain Boomer hurled a harpoon at "the old great-grandfather, with the white head and hump," but ended

up slicing off his own arm with said weapon. Ouch. Afterward, Captain Boomer was fitted with a fake arm. By happy coincidence, Captain Ahab has a fake leg (see illustration on page 37). The captains would be perfect Paralympics partners in the two-man duathlon.

Hast seen the WW? Yup, and would rather not again. Could cost an arm *and* a leg.

THE BACHELOR
Her status: Footloose and fancy-free.
Her crew: Dancing a "hilarious jig" with the "olive-hued girls who had eloped with them from the Polynesian Isles."
Her story: The *Bachelor* killed a gazillion whales. With every available barrel on the ship full to bursting with sperm oil, the crew has to use other containers—coffee cups, clothes drawers, makeup cases—to contain it all. "Everything was filled with sperm except the captain's pantaloons pockets, and those he reserved to thrust his hands into, in self-complacent testimony of his entire satisfaction." Self-satisfaction indeed. Anyway, with so much cash in the coffers, the *Bachelor* has nothing left to do but celebrate and head home to Nantucket.
Hast seen the WW? "No, only heard of him, but don't believe in him at all," the blissed-out captain tells Ahab. Then he invites Ahab and his crew to come aboard and join the party. But wet blanket Ahab refuses (of course), calls the captain "too jolly," and practically knocks the champagne glass out of his hand.

THE RACHEL
Her status: Woeful.
Her crew: Desperately seeking a lost boat.
Her story: While chasing after Moby Dick, one of the *Rachel*'s whaleboats went missing. Turns out, the captain's young son—"My boy, my own boy"—was on that boat. The stricken

captain begs Ahab to help with search and rescue, asking him to press the *Pequod* into service. "Do to me as you would have me do to you in the like case," he implores. "For you too have a boy, Captain Ahab." Ahab's reply: "I will not do it. Even now I lose time. Good bye."
Hast seen the WW? "Aye" and because she did, the *Rachel* is left "weeping for her children."

THE DELIGHT
Her status: Dejected, defeated, depleted.
Her crew: Dead in the water. Well, five of them anyway.
Her story: Brief. Sailors attack White Whale. White Whale kills sailors. The *Delight*'s captain cannot overemphasize to Ahab the futility of trying to slay Moby Dick. "The harpoon is not yet forged that will ever do that," he says. Replies Ahab, "Yeah, you're probably right." Ha! Joking!
Hast seen the WW? You know it, baby.

38
"IF I WERE A CARPENTER"

Music by Tim Harden
Lyrics by Herman Melville and The Classics Slacker

> *If I were a carpenter,*
> *and you were Captain Ahab,*
> *You would call me Carpenter.*
> *I wouldn't have a real name.*
>
> *If I worked my hands in wood,*
> *would you give me strange projects?*
> *Answer me, "Yes I would.*
> *I'd order a replacement leg."*

"Carpenter, how long before this leg is done?"
"Perhaps an hour, sir."
"Bungle away at it then, and bring it to me."

"IF I WERE A CARPENTER"

If I were a blacksmith,
working on the Pequod,
I would really hate my job,
but at least I'd have a real name [Perth].

"Often he would be surrounded by an eager circle, all waiting to be served; holding boat-spades, pikeheads, harpoons, and lances. Silent, slow, and solemn; bowing over still further his chronically broken back, he toiled away, as if toil were life itself, and the heavy beating of his hammer the heavy beating of his heart. And so it was.—Most miserable!"

If a tinker were my trade,
I wouldn't work on the Pequod.
Because Carpenter and the blacksmith, Perth
Those guys do everything.

Carpenter pulls sailors' teeth—ouch.
Carpenter drills earlobes—ouch.
Carpenter straightens sprained wrists—ouch.
Perth makes buckles and steel shoulder blades.

If I were Captain Ahab,
and you were a blacksmith,
Would you make me a special harpoon?
One for killing the White Whale that,
I've been talking about incessantly.

"One that a thousand yoke of fiends could not part, Perth; something that will stick in a whale like his own fin-bone."

Make me one with horse-shoe stubbs.
Make me one with razors.

I'll give you some of Queequeg's blood—ouch.
to temper the barbs with.

If I were a blacksmith,
and you were Captain Ahab,
I would make you a special harpoon.
One for killing the White Whale that,
You've been talking about incessantly.

One for killing the White Whale that,
You've been talking about incessantly.

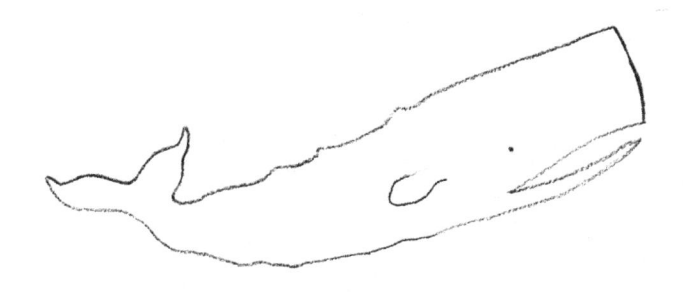

39
LET'S CALL THE
WHOLE THING OFF

*In which Ahab is struck by a brief moment of sanity
and considers going home*

Up to this point Captain Ahab has been, shall we say, single-minded. Not given to distraction. Keepin' his eye on the prize.

He never, ever has a second thought—not over the course of a million nautical miles, 133 chapters, and barrels and barrels of finger-lickin'-good sperm—that maybe, just maybe, chasing this stupid white fish for two years might be a complete waste of time. Not to mention, fatal.

He doesn't for one moment consider giving up the mission in spite of numerous warnings to abort. Not just warnings, but hints and allegations, plea bargains and arguments, supplications and omens from multitudes of people and things—plaques, soothsayers, livestock, sharks, fish, birds, hats, one-armed captains, dead sailors. Heck, the loss of his own damn leg should have indicated to Ahab that pursuing the White Whale is a REALLY BAD IDEA.

And then, finally, finally, mere hours before Moby Dick bobs to the surface within sight of the *Pequod,* a whisper of "pensive air, transparently soft" on a mild, blue-sky morning penetrates Ahab's brain in a way that all manner of flora and fauna could not. "The lovely aromas in that enchanted air did at last seem to dispel, for a moment, the cankerous thing in his soul."

Ahab slaps his gnarled, wrinkled forehead with the heel of his haggard, crackled hand and thinks, *Whoa, I might've made a big mistake here.* Not just chasing this particular beast, but forty years of whaling in general. "What a forty years' fool—fool—old fool, has old Ahab been!" A teardrop falls from one bloodshot eye into the sea.

"Oh Starbuck!" wails Ahab to his first mate. "Why this strife of the chase? Why weary, and palsy the arm at the oar, and the iron, and the lance?

"For forty years I have fed upon dry salted fare—fit emblem of the dry nourishment of my soul!—when the poorest landsman has had fresh fruit to his daily hand, and broken the world's fresh bread to my mouldy crusts."

Not only has he been eating processed and/or spoiled food, he's missed out on decades of cuddle time with Mrs. Ahab, whom he refers to as his "girl-wife," probably because he can't remember her name, although it's almost certainly Mary. Or Sarah.

"Aye, I widowed that poor girl when I married her," he bemoans. Indeed, that would be a sucky way to start a marriage. He left "but one dent" in his "marriage pillow" and "sailed for Cape Horn the next day." He made a dent in one of her ovaries, too, because she gave birth to a son. Ahab refers to him as "boy," probably because he can't remember his name, either. Noah? Jonah, maybe? (Too obvious.)

Anyway, upon hearing all this, Starbuck sees an opening and goes for it.

"Oh, my captain! my Captain! noble soul! grand old heart, after all! Why should any one give chase to that hated fish!" he cries. "Let us fly these deadly waters! let us home!" Let's turn this ship around! I have a wife waiting for me, too, at home in Nantucket, and I know for sure that her name is Mary. ("Tis my Mary! My Mary herself!") We could double-date!

You can probably guess how Ahab responds, but not in the way you might imagine. It's pretty weird, even for him: "Like a blighted fruit tree he shook, and cast his last, cindered apple to the soil." Soil? Trees? Apples? Whatever. He's not going home until he gets what he came for and Starbuck—"blanched to a corpse's hue with despair"—wanders away, leaving Ahab to babble on by himself, keening and wailing for another half a page.

He shuts up at last when he notices that Starbuck is so gone. Then Ahab spots another fellow across the deck. It is the fiendish Fedallah, the harpooneer that Ahab had hired to lead his special forces. Fedallah has one job only—to put Ahab's dark face in front of Moby Dick's white one. And that's just what he's a-gonna do.

40

LAST GASPS

In which Moby Dick sucks the air out of everyone, except Ishmael

Time to cut to "The Chase"—the climactic showdown between Captain Ahab and Moby Dick. Predictably, Ishmael takes three chapters ("The Chase—First Day"; "The Chase—Second Day"; "The Chase—Third Day") to describe what can be summarized in just a few paragraphs, à la The Classics Slacker. Here's how "The Chase" goes down:

Captain Ahab sees the object of his obsession—uh, what was it again? Oh yes, the White Whale.

He claims the gold doubloon for himself. Remember the gold doubloon? Not really? It was the sixteen-dollar coin that Ahab had nailed to the main mast, ninety-nine chapters ago, to incentivize the crew. He proclaimed that the first to spot Moby Dick would win it.

Tashtego says he saw M.D. first. Me! Me! I claim dibs!

Not so fast, counters Ahab. "Not the same instant; not the

same—no, the doubloon is mine, Fate reserved the doubloon for me. I only; none of ye could have raised the White Whale first."

But why anyone would give a flying fig about a stupid coin at this juncture is just nonsense. Doesn't anyone get that death by drowning is a real possibility here? What would they spend the money on? Does Heaven have a dry cleaners?

The whaleboats take off after Moby Dick, who turns around and charges, flinging everyone and their boats and their caps and their oars and their keys and their wallets hither and thither. Round 1, by unanimous decision, goes to the whale.

Fedallah, aka the Parsee, Ahab's chief of staff, drowns on Day 2. Which is bad enough, but the following day Ahab finds Fedallah's corpse tied to Moby Dick like a Christmas tree to the roof of a Honda Civic. "Lashed round and round to the fish's back, the half-torn body of the Parsee was seen; his sable raiment frayed to shreds; his distended eyes turned full upon old Ahab." Nasty. And a bad omen, too. Fedallah had warned Ahab: When I'm dead and you see me dead again, that's it for you big fella.

Moby Dick splits Ahab's boat in half. It's looking as if Fedallah may have been right.

Ahab somehow survives that attack, although he does get very wet and his peg leg pops off. This dismays Carpenter, as that leg represented some of his best work. Still, he's a good guy and graciously offers to make Ahab a new one, which will soon become about as useful as a gold doubloon.

Starbuck takes a last stab at trying to convince Ahab to give it up and go home: "Shall we keep chasing this murderous fish till he swamps the last man? Shall we be dragged by him to the bottom of the sea? Shall we be towed by him to the infernal world?" Yes, yes, and yes.

Moby Dick rams the *Pequod*. The three mates—Starbuck, Stubb, and Flask—make their "Alack, I die!" speeches.

Ahab throws his custom-made harpoon at Moby Dick,

which sticks in him like a toothpick in a club sandwich. As soon as it lands, the harpoon's rope catches Ahab around the neck and Moby Dick lassoes him in like a rodeo cowboy. You just don't survive something like that.

The *Pequod* begins to sink, creating a whirlpool, and everybody—from Dough-Boy to Perth, Queequeg to Pip, Tashtego to the cook, Carpenter, and the chorus line—are sucked down the drain.

Ishmael is just about to be Roto-Rootered himself when what should pop up from the vortex…Queequeg's coffin! Ishmael hops on board, much like Kate Winslet did at the end of *The Titanic*. So romantic!

Ishmael drifts along on his beloved's wooden coffin for almost 24 hours, when the *Rachel* spots him. They are hoping he's the captain's missing son, and are bitterly disappointed to discover that it's only Ishmael. With heavy hearts, they pluck him out of the water.

POSTSCRIPT

We are left to assume that Ishmael will give up whaling for a while. We do know that he travels to Peru ("let's fly away, let's float down to Peru…"), where he'll lift a glass of chicha and recount the tale of the *Town-Ho* (see "The *Town-Ho*'s Story" yet again on page 85) at a gay bar in Lima.

And that, my friends, is a good way to end a story!

THE OBLIGATORY AUTHOR BIOGRAPHY

Open any classic book and you will discover a timeline of the author's life. Do not read it. These biographies all sound the same and they always go something like this:

The Life of Herman Melville

1819: Herman Melville is born on August 1 in New York City. His father, Allan Melvill, long missing an "e" on his surname, gives one to Herman as a birthday present. It will become the most used vowel in all his future writings.

1830: Father's import business fails, forcing the family to move from Manhattan to Albany. Everybody grieves.

1832: Father dies, leaving the family in debt. Family can't even afford to live in Albany and moves to a podunk town eleven miles north.

1832-40: Melville swears, as God is his witness, that he will earn enough money to move back to Manhattan. He works for his brother (fur business), a cousin (bookkeeping), back to his brother (more fur), then to an uncle (farming). These businesses either fail or come close to failing. His brother strongly suggests Melville take a job on a whaling ship, which will keep him away from family businesses for at least four years.

1841: Melville sails from New Bedford on the whaling ship *Acushnet* (gesundheit!). He is forced to sleep with twenty men in close quarters. For the sexually impressionable Melville, it's too much of a good thing. He deserts on the Marquesa Islands, where he encounters cannibals. Fortunately, they don't have a taste for him. Sadly, neither will Nathaniel Hawthorne nine years hence.

1845: Melville writes a book, *Typee*, about his adventures on the Marquesa Islands. It is rejected by a New York publisher, but accepted by a London one. *Typee* enjoys some success, as does its sequel, *Omoo*. However, Melville's next three books—*Achoo*, *Gooey*, and *FuFu*—are commercial disasters.

1847: With enough money saved from the sale of his first two books, Melville marries Elizabeth "Lizzie" "Bessie" "Lizbeth" Shaw, the daughter of the chief justice of Massachusetts. Elizabeth chooses a private ceremony over a church wedding, in order to avoid the throngs who might come out to see the celebrity. To which Melville says, "You're a celebrity?"

1849-55: Over the course of their marriage, the Melvilles welcome four children: Malcolm "Manny" Melville; Stanwix "Stanny" Melville; Elizabeth "Libby" "Betsy" Melville; Frances "Franny" Melville.

1850: Melville meets hunky novelist Nathaniel Hawthorne at a picnic. Friendly at first, Hawthorne later turns down Melville's repeated invitations and requests to visit by telling him that he's writing, but in truth he's working on *The Scarlet Letter*. Hawthorne eventually moves to England to get away from him.

1851: *Moby Dick* is published. Despite featuring one of the largest mammals in the world with a word count to match, the book fails to make a splash. Melville dedicates it to Hawthorne "in admiration for his genius," causing Hawthorne to comment, "Wow, I wish I wasn't so smart."

1866: Per the custom of many nineteenth-century writers, Melville works as a customs house officer, a position he will hold for nineteen years. During this time, he is often quick to anger due to anxiety, pain, and drinking. Could also have been due to being a customs house officer for nineteen years.

1891: Melville succumbs to a heart attack on September 28. As if dying in obscurity isn't bad enough, *The New York Times* obituary misspells his masterpiece *Mobie Dick*. Doh!

ALSO BY THE CLASSICS SLACKER:

The Classics Slacker Reads Madame Bovary

Upcoming books in *The Classics Slacker series:*

The Classics Slacker Reads Anna Karenina
The Classics Slacker Reads The Great Gatsby
The Classics Slacker Reads Les Misérables
The Classics Slacker Reads The Picture of Dorian Gray
The Classics Slacker Reads The Scarlet Letter
The Classics Slacker Reads Silas Marner
The Classics Slacker Reads A Tale of Two Cities
The Classics Slacker Reads Ulysses
The Classics Slacker Reads War and Peace
The Classics Slacker Reads Wuthering Heights

Made in the USA
Monee, IL
08 August 2023